Bilingual and Multicultural Education:
Canadian Perspectives

Multilingual Matters

Please contact us for the latest information on recent and forthcoming books in the series.

Derrick Sharp, General Editor, Multilingual Matters,
Bank House, 8a Hill Road, Clevedon, Avon BS21 7HH, England.

MULTILINGUAL MATTERS 15

Bilingual and Multicultural Education: Canadian Perspectives

Edited by

Stan Shapson and Vincent D'Oyley

British Library Cataloguing in Publication Data

Shapson, Stan and Vincent D'Oyley (eds)
 Bilingual and multicultural education –
 (Multilingual matters; 15)
 1. Education, Bilingual — Canada
 2. Minorities -- Education — Canada
 I. Shapson, Stan   II. D'Oyley, Vincent
 III. Series
 371.97′0971   LC3734

  ISBN 0-905028-36-8
  ISBN 0-905028-35-X Pbk

Multilingual Matters Ltd,
Bank House, 8a Hill Road,
Clevedon, Avon BS21 7HH,
England.

Typeset by Wayside Graphics, Clevedon, Avon.
Printed and bound in Great Britain by
Colourways Press Ltd, Clevedon BS21 6RR.

Contents

1 Bilingual and multicultural education in Canada

Stan M. Shapson
Simon Fraser University

Abstract. As an introduction to this volume, an overview of the relationship between language policy in Canada and the education of majority and minority language students is provided. The schools' response to bilingualism is introduced with specific reference to the results of French immersion programs. The schools' response to multiculturalism focuses on the offering of different models of minority language programs, and on the recognition of multiculturalism in the general school curriculum. Future directions for educational policy are provided.

During the past fifteen years, two developments have had a dramatic effect on Canadian education. First, with the adoption of the Official Languages Act (1969), the French language gained equal rights and status with English in parliament and in all services provided by the federal government of Canada. This led to a major effort by the government to promote and stimulate instruction in Canada's two official languages, English and French. Concerns arose about the effectiveness of existing traditional French second language programs in the schools and a great deal of experimentation and innovation resulted in the development of French immersion programs. Second, there has been a vast increase in the number of immigrants to Canada, particularly among members of visible minority groups. This change in ethnic composition has challenged the schools, particularly in large urban centres, to broaden their education approaches for students from different linguistic and cultural backgrounds.

Existing publications largely deal with either bilingual or multicultural education in Canada, rarely attempting to develop both areas simultaneously. In order to best reflect features of Canadian society and government policy, the focus of the book will include a conceptualization of both bilingual and multicultural education. The main purposes are: to synthesize the recent responses to bilingualism and multiculturalism in Canadian education; to identify the issues arising out of the schools' responses to these new challenges; and to examine future directions for educational policy. For such an analysis, it is necessary to begin by distinguishing between majority and minority language students.

Majority language students are children whose first language (mother tongue) is the same as the language used by the schools as the medium of instruction (i.e. predominantly English in nine provinces and French in Quebec). These children will often have the option of learning a second language at some point in their schooling, usually on the basis of their own or their parents' choice. In Canada, this option will often be French because of the policy of bilingualism in the two official languages of Canada (see Halpern, Chapter 2; Genesee, Chapter 3).

Minority language students are children whose mother tongue (and the language predominantly spoken in their home) is not the same as the language used by the school as the medium of instruction.[1] Frequently, these students will not only be trying to cope with learning English (often without any special instruction being provided for them), but they will also be trying to learn the content of the curriculum at the same pace as their majority language peers. In teaching situations such as these, the child may receive the message, albeit subtly, that he must reject his native language and culture in school. The effects of the schools' failure to recognize the child's language and culture are revealed in the following selected quotations:

> "How much it hurts a child to have his own language ignored in a class of strangers probably never will be measured by the social scientists." (Lind, 1973: 10)

> "And there are others who, . . . are ignorant and indifferent and believe we're being very well treated for the 'class' of people we are. . . . in order to preserve the 'British way of life', they should send us all away. We're a 'lower order of people'. In one breath we are damned for being 'inassimilable' and the next there's fear that we'll assimilate." (Kogawa, 1981)

> "And now you hold out your hand and you beckon me to come across the street. Come and integrate you say. But how can I come? I am naked and ashamed. How can I come in dignity? I have no presents. I have no gifts. What is there in my culture you value? My poor treasure you can only scorn. Am I then to come

as a beggar and receive all from your omnipotent hand?" (Chief Dan George, 1971: 13)

The response of the schools to the needs of minority language children has for the most part included provisions for special instruction in the majority language (Ashworth, 1975) and the introduction of multicultural issues in the general school curriculum (see Chapters 6–9); and to a lesser extent, some minority language (non-English, non-French) programs have been offered (see Chapter 5).

Relationship between language policy and educational responses

As early as 1953 a UNESCO conference on "The Use of Vernacular Languages in Education" concluded that the best medium for teaching is the mother tongue of the pupil. This was in striking contrast to the prevailing North American "melting pot" philosophy emphasizing strong assimilation to English language and culture for minority language students. However, the debate about the proper educational condition for children whose home language differs from the language of the school continues (see Cummins, Chapter 5).

Education in Canada is a provincial jurisdiction; nevertheless, the federal presence has been very visible on wide-ranging cultural, and linguistic educational issues (Stevenson, 1981). The British North American Act of 1867 made some provisions for the English and French languages in the parliament and courts of Canada. However, it was not until 1969 that Parliament passed the Official Languages Act declaring English and French the official languages of Canada. One of the principles for the implementation of the Official Languages Act which was approved by parliamentary resolution in 1973 had dramatic significance for bilingual education:

"Subject to circumstances which may make a deferment of application necessary, Canadians have a right to have their children educated in the official language of their choice, and the necessary facilities should be provided wherever numbers warrant."

It is also important to note that the federal government's Royal Commission Report on Bilingualism and Multiculturalism (1970) made specific recommendations that had the potential to significantly affect the education of *minority* students not represented by the two official language groups. Two of these recommendations were as follows:

"We recommend that the teaching of languages other than English and French and cultural subjects related to them, be incorporated as options in the public elementary school program, where there is sufficient demand for such classes."

"We recommend that special instruction in the appropriate official language be provided for children who enter the public school system with an inadequate knowledge of that language."

Subsequently, the federal government announced a policy of "multiculturalism in a bilingual framework" (House of Commons Debates, 1971).

As previously indicated, provincial policy has to assume a major role in language education in Canada. In some cases clauses of the Schools Administration Act governing languages used in teaching have been quite specific. For example, a sample of a section under duties of teachers in one province stated:

(e) in instruction and in all communications with the pupils . . .

(i) to use the English language, except where it is impractical to do so by reason of the pupil not understanding English, and except in respect of instruction in a language other than English when such other language is being taught as one of the subjects in the course of study, or

(ii) to use the French language in schools or classes in which French is the language of instruction . . .
(quoted in Toronto Board of Education, 26 April 1973)

In the 1970s a few of the provinces of western Canada whose legislation was restrictive with regard to languages of instruction officially amended their education acts to permit instruction in languages other than English and French in the schools. Consequently, some school systems did incorporate minority languages as the media of instruction for part of the curriculum (see Cummins, Chapter 5).

The schools' response to bilingualism

Over the past fifteen years, the number and diversity of educational opportunities for majority English-speaking children to learn French as a second language have greatly increased (see Halpern, Chapter 2). This has been prompted by the desire of many Canadians for the improvement and strengthening of French language instruction, and has been stimulated by federal funding to encourage innovation and research in bilingual education. Of the variety of programs which have resulted, *immersion* appears to be among the most effective for enabling English-speaking children to attain high levels of proficiency in French (see Genesee, Chapter 3).

Immersion is very different from the traditional French second language (FSL) approach in which French is taught as a separate subject, for about 20–30 minutes per day. An immersion program involves a switch of languages between the home and the school. Initially *all* or at least a very significant part of the curriculum is taught using the children's second language (French) as the language of instruction. French language instruction (i.e. the explicit teaching of vocabulary and grammatical rules) is not necessarily excluded from the immersion classroom, but the opportunity that immersion provides for children to learn language through its use rather than through explicit instruction is its distinguishing feature (Genesee, Chapter 3; Stern, 1978).

The most well known type of immersion program is *early total immersion*, which begins in kindergarten or grade one with children receiving their first two or three years of schooling with French as the *only* language of instruction. English language instruction (the child's first language) is *not* introduced until grade two or three. With each successive grade, the proportion of time in which English is used is increased, so that by the end of elementary school the curriculum is approximately balanced between English and French instruction.

The first immersion program was implemented in the majority French-speaking province of Quebec (Lambert & Tucker, 1972). Immersion programs have quickly spread to other parts of the country and now operate in every Canadian province. A considerable amount of research has been conducted on early immersion programs across Canada (e.g. Genesee, Chapter 3; Lambert & Tucker, 1972; Shapson & Day, 1982; Swain, Lapkin & Andrew, 1981). Briefly, this research has consistently demonstrated that children enrolled in these programs:

(a) are not harmed in their cognitive or native language (i.e. English) development;

(b) master content subjects (e.g. mathematics, science) as well as their unilingually educated peers; and

(c) develop high levels of proficiency in French.

More specifically, findings from these studies have shown that in the primary grades, immersion children generally lag behind their peers in the regular English program on tests of English language arts. However, these early lags tend to close soon after English language instruction is introduced into the curriculum, and by grade four, any discrepancies found between immersion and regular program students have disappeared. With regard to proficiency in French, comparisons between immersion students and those enroled in more traditional FSL programs have shown that immersion children attain consistently higher levels of performance. Comparisons with native Francophone children have therefore served as a more meaningful reference point. These comparisons have revealed that immersion children attain native Francophone levels in receptive or more passive language skills (reading, listening comprehension), but still show many non-native characteristics in the productive language skills (speaking and writing) (Spilka, 1976; Harley & Swain, 1978).

No other Canadian educational innovation has been so thoroughly researched and successfully replicated across the country. As a result of the success of immersion programs, Canada is providing leadership in language education. In Chapter 3, Genesee presents a detailed review of the findings of immersion programs.

The schools' response to multiculturalism

Language education and the minority child

Throughout North America, the primary (and in many cases the only) response of the schools to the minority language child has been to provide special instruction in the majority language (e.g. English, see Ashworth, 1975; Saville-Troike, 1976). Since it has been widely acknowledged that the minority language child has to adjust to both a different language and culture, the general aims of these programs have come to include not only sufficient teaching in the majority language so that the student can take his place in regular school programs; but also providing him with help and understanding so that he can quickly enter the culture of the school and the outside world.

Different approaches for the example of English as a second language (ESL) have been reviewed by Ashworth (1975). Some educators feel that young children profit from *total integration* (placement in a regular class immediately upon arrival), and for this reason some schools offer no special English language training. At the other end of the spectrum, *reception classes* composed entirely of students who require intensive ESL training by a specialist teacher, or *withdrawal classes*, where the student spends part of the time in his homeroom class and the remaining time in the ESL class, are commonly found in many school districts.

But what about educational approaches for minority language children which have a broader focus than special instruction in the majority language? According to Cummins:

"The most contentious issues in policy debates in virtually all the western industrialized countries has been whether, and to what extent the home language (L1) of minority group children should be incorporated into the school curriculum." (Chapter 5)

Cummins thoroughly reviews the theoretical issues surrounding the offering of minority languages in the schools and presents models of minority language programs in terms of assumptions regarding their significance for either *transitional* or *enrichment* purposes.

The rationale for *transitional* minority language programs is that, in those cases where minority group children encounter academic difficulties, it is a consequence of the mismatch between the language/culture of the home and that of the school. In a transition program, the mother tongue is used as a *temporary* bridge to facilitate subsequent instruction in English. Its main aim is to make the minority child's adjustment to school more secure while not retarding his academic progress during the learning of the majority laguage (i.e. English). Although *two* languages are used initially in the classroom, the goals of the program involve learning only one language, *English*. An example of a transition program is that offered during the early school years in Toronto for Italian children (Shapson & Purbhoo, 1977).

On the other hand, the rationale underlying programs for *enrichment* purposes is the enrichment or development of a minority language. Enrichment minority language programs are based on the desire of ethnic group members to have their children retain their language and its associated group identity and culture. They believe that language is the vehicle for transmitting their culture and thereby fostering a sense of self-esteem, ethnic identity, and pride in their children. Examples of programs of this nature in Canada are two relatively large-scale initiatives, the Heritage Language Programme in Ontario and the Programme d'Enseignement Langues d'Origins in Quebec (see Cummins, Chapter 5), and some smaller scale programs, the Hebrew–English–French trilingual programs in Montreal (Genesee, Tucker & Lambert, 1978) and the Ukrainian–English bilingual programs in Alberta schools (e.g. Muller, Penner, Blowers, Jones & Mosychuk, 1977).

Another model of a language program for enrichment occurs when both majority and minority language groups are simultaneously learning two languages. This "two way" approach can be found in California; half the students are native speakers of Spanish (who have no option but to become bilingual in English/Spanish) and the other half are English-speaking American children whose parents, by opting for the program, display a desire to have their children become bilingual (Engle, 1975).

Recognition of multiculturalism in the general school curriculum

A useful definition of "multicultural education" is that given by Thomas L. Wells in the Legislature of Ontario Debates:

"It is an education in which the individual child of whatever origin finds, not mere acceptance or tolerance, but respect and understanding. It is an education in which cultural diversity is seen and used as a valuable resource to enrich the lives of all. It is an education in which differences and similarities are used for positive ends. It is an education in which every child has the chance to benefit from the cultural heritage of others as well as his or her own." (Quoted in Michalski, 1977: 81)

The above definition can serve as a reminder that, apart from language education, the schools should also attempt to recognize multiculturalism in the general school curriculum for the benefit of all students from both *majority* and *minority* groups. Strong support for the recognition of multiculturalism in the general school curriculum is born out in a recent survey in British Columbia involving 237 central office personnel in 70 school districts. Day & Shapson (1981) found that nearly all respondents were in favour of programs and activities pertaining to multiculturalism in the general school curriculum; however, only about 20% were supportive of including minority languages as the medium of instruction for at least part of the curriculum.

A few selected examples of the schools' response to multicultural approaches for all students are introduced below. Some significant developments in this area are then elaborated upon (Chapters 6–9). Also, Anderson (1982) has proposed new directions for theory and research on minority groups in Canada that are of central importance for educators developing multicultural curricula.

Multicultural curriculum units. Subjects in the curriculum, particularly social studies, often include units dealing with multicultural issues, such as ethnic histories, life-styles, customs and values. Recently, however, concerns have arisen with the most common approach adopted, the "tourist or museum approach":

"Student understanding of ethnic groups and issues is organized around artifacts and interesting 'facts' through which he is taken as a tourist . . . He colours teepees, draws igloos, eats curried rice and listens to ethnic songs . . . this approach to people tends to ignore the conceptual understandings, issues and cultural meanings which underlie the objects students look at." (Werner, 1979: 2–3)

While a museum approach may be useful to stimulate student interest in other cultures, a number of researchers have argued for the creation of a more comprehensive curriculum design (e.g. Banks, 1976; Bramwell, 1981; Werner, Connors, Aoki & Dahlie, 1980). To meet this challenge, Connors (Chapter 7) provides the basis for the construction of a multicultural curriculum within a critical reflective process. Wright & LaBar (Chapter 8) view multiculturalism as a moral concern; they develop a theoretical framework for multicultural education based on moral principles.

Racism. There is no shortage of literature that speaks of racism and stereotyping in schools (see Kehoe & Echols, Chapter 9). A concentrated effort is now going into the development of materials and programs which correct biases and omissions of the past and attempt to promote cross-cultural understanding. The first comprehensive approach toward race relations was introduced by the Toronto Board of Education:

> "Many people argue that we 'can't legislate attitudes' and that therefore we cannot combat racism. It is true that in our society it is not possible to legislate the way people feel and think. But it is possible to offer them assistance and incentives to change their attitudes. And it is certainly possible, especially in a school system, to regulate behavior, and to create the kind of structures that act strongly against racism and strongly in favour of tolerance. Our hope is that once people get used to the fact that racist behavior will not be tolerated, the appropriate attitude change will follow." (D. Barr, Chairman, Sub-Committee on Race Relations, Toronto Board of Education, 29 May 1978)

The Sub-Committee then developed 159 specific recommendations for combatting racism in every sphere, ranging from curriculum, placement and assessment of students, extracurricular activities, system sensitivity, and teacher hiring practices. Some other school systems have lately emulated this pattern with their own policies and programs; for example, see May & Filipoff (1982) for "Vancouver Perspectives". While it is perhaps too soon to evaluate the effectiveness of these programs, one can agree that they are an encouraging change from the more common approach in the past, which has been to ignore instances of racism in the schools and hope that they go away. Further promising educational strategies for combatting racism and stereotyping are discussed by Buchignani (1982) and Kehoe & Echols (Chapter 9).

Future directions for educational policy

This is an exciting time to be an educator involved in bilingual and multicultural education in Canada. The new Canadian Constitution incorporates a Charter of Rights and Freedom which reaffirms and extends the status and use of Canada's two official languages; and it supports a policy of preservation and enhancement of the multicultural heritage of Canada, such as reinforcing protection against discrimination and preserving the right to use languages other than English and French (Constitution Act, 1982).

What is on the horizon for bilingual and multicultural education in Canada? The adoption of the Charter of Rights and Freedom creates a new opportunity for educational replanning and further integration of bilingual and multicultural curriculum and policy. "Future Directions for Educational Policy" will be addressed in Chapters 10–11.

While studies conducted up to the early 1960s seemed to provide data which suggested harmful effects of bilingualism, they suffered from severe methodological problems (see Peal & Lambert, 1967). For more recent well-designed studies, one can look to immersion programs (Genesee, Chapter 3), and minority language programs (Cummins, Chapter 5) as examples. They clearly demonstrate that children can indeed learn two languages in school. One implication of this finding is that parent and community groups may be requesting that more languages be offered in the curriculum. Halpern (1979) has reminded us that schools are labour intensive; they provide jobs for many groups of people, the largest single group being teachers. The offering of language programs in the schools may create a situation in which the legitimate needs of teachers as a labour force conflict with the legitimate needs of students as a consumer group. Bilingual and multicultural programming in the future will have major consequences for policy makers, particularly with regard to the hiring of new teachers and the development of responsive teacher education programs.

In order to make predictions about the future of language policy in Canadian education, Tucker (Chapter 10) suggests that it is important to look beyond the boundary of Canada and consider the international experience. Tucker examines the approaches in several developing countries, in the United States, and in the People's Republic of China as a means of analyzing the future development of language policy relevant to the Canadian situation.

How may we better ensure responsiveness to multicultural education which, along with the official policy of bilingualism, reinforces the cultural richness of the varied minority groups in the Canadian mosaic? In 1965, Porter illustrated, what many minority leaders understand and have well expressed, that many groups are not equal in their access to the political structures of Canadian society. In the concluding Chapter, D'Oyley proposes a way of viewing our already developed system within our government whose structures should begin to respond to five main groups (Aboriginal, Anglophone, Francophone, later European, later Visible Minorities) when formulating further policy. Only time will tell if this departure will be realized.

Notes to Chapter One

1. The term "minority" might be misleading in certain situations because students in this group might constitute a numerical majority in some schools.

References

ANDERSON, A. B. 1982, Canadian ethnic studies: Traditional preoccupations and new directions. *Journal of Canadian Studies*, 17, 5–15.

ASHWORTH, M. 1975, *Immigrant children and Canadian schools*. Toronto: McClelland & Stewart.

BANKS, J. A. 1976, Ethnic studies as a process of curriculum reform. *Social Education*, 40, 76–80.

BARR, D. 1978, Draft Report of the Sub-Committee on Race Relations. Toronto: Board of Education for the City of Toronto, May 29.

BRAMWELL, R. D. 1981, The semantics of multiculturalism: A new element in curriculum. *Canadian Journal of Education*, 6, 92–102.

BUCHIGNANI, N. 1982, Practical strategies to foster inter-racial harmony through the educational system. In V. D'OYLEY (ed.), *Perspectives on race, education and social development: Emphasis on Canada*. Vancouver: University of British Columbia, Centre for the Study of Curriculum and Instruction.

CONSTITUTION ACT 1982, *Charter of rights and freedom*. Ottawa: Government of Canada.

DAY, E. & SHAPSON, S. 1981, *Multiculturalism: A survey of school districts in British Columbia*. Burnaby, B.C.: Simon Fraser University. July.

ENGLE, P. 1975, Language medium in early school years for minority language groups. *Review of Educational Research*, 45, 283–325.

GENESEE, F., TUCKER, R. & LAMBERT, W. 1978, An experiment in trilingual education. *The Canadian Modern Language Review*, 34, 621–43.

GEORGE, CHIEF DAN. 1971, Dramatic soliloquy. *Curriculum Bulletin* (Manitoba Department of Youth and Education), 6, 13–14.

HALPERN, G. 1979, Sociopolitics and second language teaching programs. Burnaby, B.C.: Simon Fraser University, Site Lecture Series. July.

HARLEY, B. & SWAIN, M. 1978, An analysis of the verb system used by young learners of French. *Interlanguage Studies Bulletin*, 3, 35–79.

HOUSE OF COMMONS DEBATES. 1971, Ottawa: Government of Canada, October 8, 1971.

KOGAWA, J. 1981, *Obasan*. Toronto: Lester & Orpen Dennys Ltd.

LAMBERT, W. & TUCKER, R. 1972, *Bilingual education of children: The St. Lambert experiment*. Rowley, Mass.: Newbury House.

LIND, L. 1973, New Canadianism: Melting the ethnics in Toronto schools. *This Magazine*, 7, 6–10.

MAY, E. & FILIPOFF, S. 1982, Racism or multiculturalism: Vancouver perspectives. In V. D'OYLEY (ed.), *Perspectives on race, education and social development: Emphasis on Canada*. Vancouver: University of British Columbia, Centre for the Study of Curriculum and Instruction.

MICHALSKI, C. 1977, Teacher education for a multicultural society: Some global trends and the Ontario Ministry of Education position. In V. D'OYLEY (ed.), *The impact of multi-ethnicity on Canadian education*. Toronto: The Urban Alliance on Race Reations.

MULLER, L., PENNER, W., BLOWERS, T., JONES, J. & MOSYCHUK, H. 1977, Evaluation of a bilingual (English-Ukrainian) program. *The Canadian Modern Language Review*, 33, 476–85.

OFFICIAL LANGUAGES ACT. 1969, Ottawa: Government of Canada.

PEAL, E. & LAMBERT, W. 1967, The relation of bilingualism to intelligence. In J. MICHEL (ed.), *Foreign language teaching: An anthology*. New York: Macmillan.

PORTER, J. 1965, The vertical mosaic: An analysis of social class and power in Canada. Toronto: University of Toronto Press.

ROYAL COMMISSION REPORT. 1970, *Bilingualism and Multiculturalism Book 4: The Contributions of other ethnic groups*. Ottawa: Queen's Printer.

SAVILLE-TROIKE, M. 1976, *Foundations for teaching English as a second language*. Englewood Cliffs, N.J.: Prentice-Hall.

SHAPSON, S. & DAY, E. 1982, A longitudinal evaluation of an early immersion program in British Columbia. *Journal of Multilingual & Multicultural Development*, 3, 1–16.

SHAPSON, S. & PURBHOO, M. 1977, A transition program for Italian children. *The Canadian Modern Language Review*, 33, 486–96.

SPILKA, I. 1976, Assessment of second language performance in immersion programs. *The Canadian Modern Language Review*, 32, 543–61.

STERN, H. H. 1978, French immersion in Canada: Achievement and directions. *The Canadian Modern Language Review*, 34, 836–54.

STEVENSON, H. A. 1981, The federal presence in Canadian education, 1939–1980. In J. W. G. IVANY & M. E. MANLEY-CASIMIR (eds), *Federal-provincial relations: Education Canada*. Toronto: OISE Press.

SWAIN, M., LAPKIN, S. & ANDREW, C. 1981, Early French immersion later on. *Journal of Multilingual & Multicultural Development*, 2, 1–23.

TORONTO BOARD of EDUCATION. 1973, Report of the educating new Canadians Committee: A foreign language as a transitional language of instruction (Section C). Toronto: The Board of Education for the City of Toronto. April 26.

UNESCO. 1953, *The use of vernacular languages in education*. Monographs on fundamental education, No. 8. Paris: UNESCO.

WERNER, W. 1979, The ethnic factor and curriculum. Paper presented at the Canadian Ethnic Studies Association, Biennial Conference, Vancouver, B.C. October 11.

WERNER, W., CONNORS, B., AOKI, T. & DAHLIE, J. 1980, *Whose culture? Whose heritage? Ethnicity within Canadian social studies curricula.* Vancouver: University of British Columbia, Centre for the Study of Curriculum and Instruction.

The Schools' Response to Bilingualism

2 Second language teaching programs

Gerald Halpern
Department of Secretary of State

Abstract. Four categories of school-based second language programs are examined: core, extended, immersion, and submersion. Each is described in terms of designated time patterns, use of time, and teaching strategies. Reasons why non-Anglophone Canadians study English and why non-Francophone Canadians study French are presented together with the likely consequences for each of acquiring an additional language. This chapter concludes with a brief review of the financial and social costs of providing and of not providing second language teaching programs. The suggestion made is that all Canadian students should have an equal opportunity to acquire a second language.

This chapter examines Second Language Teaching Programs; not Second Language Learning Programs. This distinction allows me to discuss questions concerning their establishment (why?), location (where?), time of origin (when?), and their clientele (for whom?). Occasionally, I will refer to methods of language teaching because the methods strongly influence the learning in these language classes. But teaching will not always result in learning. The converse is equally true; much learning may take place without explicit teaching. Much knowledge of the history of language programs is not necessary in order to recognize that most language learning occurs when individuals find themselves in a lesser power position with regard to some group or individual that speaks a different language. Inhabitants of a country which has been successfully invaded have invariably found it necessary to learn the language of the conquerers. The same situation has occurred each time people left their home country or region and moved to another with a different language. Clearly then much language learning takes place without teaching programs. The motivation created by a dominant group speaking a different language than one's own has accounted for more language learning than any other reason, including second language teaching programs.

Second language teaching programs are to be found in situations where people are learning languages for reasons other than necessity. One reason of particular importance in Canada is the fact that in 1969 the federal government, with the support of all political parties, adopted the Official Languages Act. This Act gave equality of status and of language rights to both English and French, in respect to all institutions of Parliament and all services provided by the federal government. This has had important implications in areas of the country with a significant number of official minority language speakers. It has provided the public with access to federal services in both English and French. It has also meant that the public service has had a need to employ workers who speak both official languages. This led to a great demand for federal public servants capable of using both of Canada's official languages and the need for bilingual persons was to be met by the federal government providing second language training for their public servants. The high enrolment of public servants made these programs the largest of their kind in the world. Some of the enrolees did so because they were coerced; others for reasons of economic self interest. Many entered the programs with a belief that the acquisition of a second language would provide intimate access into a second culture. These three reasons (basic necessity, a means of economic improvement, an entry to another culture) are the major reasons for second language teaching programs. Their relative importance differs across language learners and across language learning situations.

Many discussions of why people learn a second language ignore the reasons which we define as basic necessity. The other two reasons, economic advantage and cultural orientation, are the ones most frequently recognized, not only in Canada but in other countries as well. For example, an official brochure designed to implement a language policy in Ireland contains the following: "Although motives of language learners are rarely unmixed, it is possible to distinguish between two types of motivation: learning a language for the social and material advancement to be gained, and learning a language because of an interest in, a favourable attitude toward, or a wish to be part of a different cultural-linguistic group."

In addition to the three reasons cited above a fourth reason is the focus of some recent research. It might not be included as an acceptable reason, for as yet we have neither extensive research evidence to substantiate it nor a sufficient number of individual language learners citing it as their motive for language acquisition. This fourth reason is based on the hypothesis that the balanced bilingual may have greater cognitive flexibility and superior ability in concept formation than does the monolingual. Some suggestions along these lines were reported as early as 1967 by Peal & Lambert. This hypothesis is discussed in greater detail by Cummins (see Chapter 4).

This paper focuses on second language teaching programs in Canada, in particular the teaching of French as a second language. This is the more common situation in the nine provinces of Canada where French is the official minority language.

Although reference is always made to *second* language for the additional language to be acquired, we must recognize that for many people the language being acquired may be a third or a fourth language. We should also recognize that the term foreign language teaching is also used as well as second language teaching. Foreign language teaching was the more frequent phrase until about the mix-sixties when, mostly for political reasons, the term second language teaching began to supplant it. Second language teaching programs are often oriented to the acquisition of another language for the purpose of *direct* communication — speaking and understanding the spoken language. Foreign language teaching often connotes *indirect* communication — reading and writing in an additional, usually a non-official, language.

The following section provides a review of the four major approaches to second language teaching programs in the schools (core, extended, immersion and submersion) and their relationships to the reasons why such programs are provided.

Major approaches to second language teaching programs

The core approach, the traditional French second language program, seeks to develop on the part of the student an ability to understand, read, speak and write the target language up to some specified level. It typically involves study of the second language itself for x minutes per day, y days per week, beginning at a defined grade level (Tucker, 1974). In Canada, this is typically 20 minutes a day for five days beginning around grade five or six. The range is anywhere from about 60 to 200 minutes per week. Within this general framework, widely different teaching or organizational strategies are used. Many of the programs use a grammar translation method in which the student is explicitly taught rules of grammar, and is asked to memorize basic lists of vocabularly, case endings, verb conjugations, and so forth. More recently, in the last thirty years that approach has been changing and the audio-lingual method has begun to replace it. With this method, students are introduced to the target language by a teacher who has native or near native command of it. The students listen to, repeat, practice, and then expand on what the teacher says. Students are introduced orally to basic vocabulary and to grammatical structures which they then practice in class. The audio-lingual approach is now the dominant one for core French language teaching in Canada.

The extended approach is a combination of a core language teaching program plus the study of a content area through the medium of the second language. This approach typically involves the introduction at an early grade of the core program, followed by the use of the target language at a later grade level to teach a specific subject area (e.g. geography or social studies). Underlying this approach is the assumption that the subject area will be mastered as well through the medium of the second language as it would have been taught in the student's first language. By studying the subject in the second language, the acquisition of the second language will be enhanced by the functional use to which it is being put.

The third approach is known as immersion and it typically involves the exclusive use of the target language in the school at the initial grade levels. Early total immersion begins with kindergarten, grade one and grade two being taught 100% through the second language. Across grade levels, the percentage of time for the first and second languages will change so that by the end of elementary school, schooling will be half in English and half in French. Immersion does not always begin at the primary level. There are variations of immersion where students begin schooling in their mother tongue and then an immersion program is instituted at the junior level, at the intermediate level, or even at the high school level (see Genesee, Chapter 3).

The fourth approach is that of submersion where an individual child is placed into a second language classroom together with students from whom the language of the classroom is their first language. This approach to learning French as a second language is relatively common in the province of Quebec and is also available in limited ways in New Brunswick and Manitoba. It is also found in all provinces of Canada where students of a non-official language background arrive and are submerged in an English language classroom where they are expected to acquire English as their second language.

Earlier it was stated that much learning can take place without explicit teaching. The submersion approach, whether it is in or outside the classroom, is not language teaching but nonetheless much language learning occurs. The core approach is structured teaching although learning does not always occur. Second language learning requires not only a particular approach; it also requires an appropriate strategy. According to Stern (1978) two basic strategies are available: the formal and the functional. The formal strategy uses language study with only limited opportunity for practice. The functional strategy requires the actual meaningful use of the language.

The four approaches described above vary with respect to the degree to which they use formal and functional strategies. The typical core program uses almost an entirely formal strategy. Extended programs use a combination of formal and functional strategies with the stress being on the formal aspects of language. The immersion program uses largely the functional strategies although it too must include a great deal of formal language teaching. The submersion situation is mostly a language use approach without any prior language study or language practice.

Why second language teaching programs?

The four approaches to second language teaching provide programs for students motivated by necessity, economics, and cultural attractions. These motivations can be personalized to provide an understanding of why non-Anglophones study English and non-Francophones study French.

Second language learning has major advantages. Some are more obvious; others quite surprising. In 1970, a survey was taken of a non-systematic sample of 100 Anglophone parents in the Ottawa-Carleton region, who had enroled their children in the very first classes of French immersion at the kindergarten level. Their reasons for doing so clustered into four groups. One group consisted of the economic reasons, a second language would be instrumental in getting a better job. A second and equally important group of reasons was the feeling that educated people speak more than one language. This reason, which is an elitist reason, is also typically a non-North American reason. The third group of reasons was somewhat different. One of the families surveyed felt that by putting children into an immersion program they would ensure a more challenging education for them. The fourth group of reasons was more altruistic. Some of the people questioned felt that as Canada does have two official languages, and a vibrant French culture worth understanding, an immersion program might be the way to learn about them.

These four groups of reasons, given by Anglophone parents, differed from the reasons found in Quebec where English is taught as a second language.

In the province of Quebec, 60% of the people are unilingual French, 10% unilingual English, and about 30% speak both English and French. Historically of these 30%, most had to learn English as a second language. Among French-speaking Quebecois, 64% work exclusively in French, 3% work exclusively in English, and 32% work in both languages. Almost one-third of French-speaking Quebecois have learned English as a second language. The pressure toward bilingualism is powerful in Quebec. In other provinces, the pressure for Francophones to learn English is even more powerful, but the motives are mixed. The French Canadian has an additional factor to take into account when he considers learning his other official language. English Canadians learning French are members of a majority group, attempting to learn a second language, and all of the reasons for doing so are reasons that will be of benefit to them. The French Canadian learning English not only recognizes that his second language will be an advantage — he recognizes that for him the language is a necessity. He must learn it unless he is to restrict himself to rather narrow regions within North America. The French Canadian *also* knows that, outside the province of Quebec, the learning of English can become the first step toward assimilation. The Francophone's first language is constantly being threatened by the overwhelming presence of English and it is a struggle to prevent it from being engulfed. This presence is felt even in areas such as Ottawa, where there is a large concentration of French Canadians and where there are strong federal institutions to protect both language groups. It is certainly much more difficult in British Columbia or Newfoundland for a person of French language heritage to retain his language and culture.

When school programs available to students from minority groups are examined, it is found that the French Canadian has good reason to fear such assimilation. In general, schools either ignore the minority language by submerging the minority group student into the majority language or they make temporary use of the minority language as a transition language. This transition use, particularly common in the United States (Cummins, Chapter 5; Engle, 1975), is also found in several places across Canada. Two examples are the Punjabi program for Punjab children in Vancouver, and the Italian program for students of Italian origin in Toronto (Shapson & Purbhoo, 1977). Such programs are intended to ease the child's transition from the immigrant family's language to the language of the majority culture, by placing the kindergarten or grade one child in a class where the teacher and other children speak the minority language. Shapson & Purbhoo (1977), studying the transition program in Toronto, summarized some of their observations by noting that the program has been bilingual only because two languages have been used in the classroom. The educational goals, however, involved learning only one language — English. Shapson & Purbhoo also observed that the children seemed aware that English was the language of the school. The message that English was the important language became stronger as the program continued from one grade to the next. Programs such as this follow in the tradition of a melting pot approach to education in which all cultures are to be homogenized into a single national culture. It is not an approach that has appealed to minority group members who want their children to retain their first language and its associated group identity and culture. It is very clear, from the presentations made to the Toronto Work Group on Multicultural Programs (Toronto Board of Education, 1975), that the non-official language groups ask that their culture, history and language be preserved in order that they may communicate with their own children. But they also want their children to have a sense of identity, history and pride, without hindering the learning of the majority language of the society.

The same kinds of concerns are expressed by French Canadians in minority situations in British Columbia, Alberta, Ontario and Saskatchewan, and by Acadians in the Maritimes.

The motives of language learners are one part of the answer to "why?" second language teaching programs are necessary. The other part is the aspiration level for language acquisition. What level of proficiency is intended as a result of a particular second language teaching program? Three aspiration levels, as defined by the Gillin Report (Ontario Ministry of Education, 1974), are provided here because they are not only useful definitions, but they have also became very widespread. The *basic level* is reached when the student has a good fundamental knowledge of the language, a basic vocabulary a minimum number of basic sentence structures, and can make himself understood in conversation, even if it is with some difficulty. The *middle level* allows the person to read books of personal interest, to read newspapers with occasional help from the dictionary, and to be able to understand radio and television programs in which he is personally interested. He can participate adequately in a conversation. The *top level* is a level at which the student can take further education in a French language institution. The person has a sufficient command of the second language so that he could accept training or employment in the other language, and participate comfortably in a community in which everyone else spoke only the second language. These three goal levels or aspiration levels require different second language teaching programs. Different aspiration levels are implicit in the various motives for second language learning. If all that is required is the ability to move comfortably as a tourist in the other language community, then the basic level is sufficient. In fact, the basic level of French is often called "tourist French".

The middle level would be far more comfortable for the Anglophone living in a city such as Montreal, and the top level is, of course, a necessity if one aspires to live in the culture associated with the other language.

The use of the basic and middle levels is generally restricted to simple situations, such as being a tourist in a community which speaks the other language. Although this is a very functional use of the language, it is difficult to believe that language learning would stop at that level, except for individuals who move as tourists in and out of the other language community. Any sustained exposure to the second language, any opportunity to practice and actively use the other language, would soon move the proficiency to higher levels.

Where to obtain second language teaching programs?

The "where?" question can begin to be answered with a consideration of language study (formal strategy) and language practice (functional strategy). Most second language teaching programs use formal strategies because core teaching is far more prevalant than either the extended or immersion approach. Second language teaching programs using the formal strategies are available throughout Canada; and a book titled "Where to Learn French or English" (Secretary of State, 1979) indicates all the institutions, both private and public, which offer language training, as well as the amount of time provided for each course and the cost. Beyond these formal schools, there is the full range of books, magazines, periodicals, records, and radio and television shows that are more or less available to Canadians attempting to learn a second language. Both English and French television and radio have become widespread across Canada, although there still are a few localities where these media are not available in both languages.

The functional strategy for second language learning presupposes some prior basic learning. Two types of situations using the functional strategy include: the use of the second language in one's own community, and the use of the language in exchanges. It is important to consider the relationship between the language of the community and success in language teaching programs. Many people, particularly those in the western provinces expect that immersion programs will be more successful in bilingual cities such as Montreal or in Ottawa-Hull than in unilingual areas. However, this does not appear to be the case. Evaluations have shown quite clearly that immersion programs can be as highly successful in unilingual as in bilingual environments in Canada (e.g. Swain, 1981). The reason why a bilingual location does not appear to confer any advantages is that, for the most part, children in immersion programs tend to make relatively little use of opportunities for using French outside of the school. The only television programs they are likely to watch on a French channel are hockey games or cartoons. In both cases, the visual image is, to a large extent, independent of the verbal accompaniment. However, studies indicate that although children in immersion programs tend not to actively seek out opportunities to use French outside the school, they do feel relatively comfortable in situations where they are required to use French (e.g. Cziko, Lambert, Sidoti & Tucker, 1980). In contrast, children in core French programs tend to feel threatened by such situations.

Although a bilingual environment is not a prerequisite for language learning, it is true that such an environment, coupled with an expectation for language learning, provides excellent opportunity for the use of the functional strategy. During the 1950s, the city of Montreal was linguistically divided; the vast majority of Anglophone Montrealers neither spoke French nor expected to speak French. The opportunity was there, but not the expectation. That situation has changed drastically. The Montreal of the 1970s was an environment in which the Anglophone expected to learn French and he did learn French.

In an exchange program, the second language learner is given the opportunity to speak the second language in a community other than that of his home. At the national level, there exist a number of programs organized by the Council of Ministers of Education. There are also other organizations working in this area such as the Canadian Council of Christians and Jews, and the Society for Educational Visits and Exchanges in Canada. Exchanges of this kind are not new. They have been organized in Canada for over 45 years and have been functioning in other countries for even longer. There is a great deal of research available on these programs (Desrochers & Clement, 1979). Also, simulated exchanges hold promise, on a cost-effectiveness basis, of providing extensive language practice and therefore the potential of extensive language learning. There are a variety of technological means for simulating exchanges. Something as simple as a letter is one such method of non-physical exchange that involves communication. It may, however, not be a favoured method because the audio-lingual method, which is presently being extensively used, does not favour written communication. However, there is conceptually no reason why telephone exchanges and even video-tape exchanges, are not possible. In relation to the cost of physically sending a group of students from Vancouver to Quebec city for a one-week exchange, the cost of purchasing a videotape machine in each school, in order to have exchanges via television, would be a far less expensive procedure.

Another procedure is the creation of a simulated visit to a second language environment within a school. One example of a simulated exchange is found in Dade County, Florida, and it involves a one-week immersion in the Spanish language. But this is not immersion in the same sense that our Canadian French immersion programs operate. In the Dade County School, one classroom was designed as a Spanish Centre, and it was appropriately decorated and furnished for that purpose. Only Spanish was spoken and the students underwent a short term, six-day immersion experience. The sixth day, Saturday, is spent with a Spanish-speaking family. The school system reports great success in terms of language learning using this functional strategy.

When to introduce second language teaching programs?

At what age or grade level should second language teaching be introduced? A longitudinal study of second language learning which followed large groups of students in Britain reached two conclusions (Burstall, Jamieson, Cohen & Hargreaves, 1974). These were, that time mattered most in language learning and furthermore, given the same amount of time, older learners were more efficient language learners than younger ones. This finding by the Burstall group was counter to earlier views (Penfield, 1967), but in agreement with the findings of a study of teaching French as a foreign language in eight countries as reported by Carroll (1975). Many Canadian educators provided counter arguments to the Burstall findings. Yet it must be noted that the research in Canada, and the opinions of Canadian educators and the general public, all seem to have reached a similar conclusion. A small amount of oral French given once a day over a period of two or three years in the elementary schools does not lead to any *substantial* gain in the ability to speak French for those who start early when compared to those who start later. At the same time, however, we must be careful not to generalize from this study which speaks directly to the formal teaching of language for brief periods of time each day, to either the extended approach, or to the immersion approach, both of which go beyond formal teaching and capitalize on language use strategies.

The major question really reduces to whether or not children learn a second language any better or more easily than adults. The weight of the evidence supports the position that in many respects, the young child is neither as efficient nor as successful in learning a second language as is the older individual. Subtle language characteristics such as accent and intonation are ignored in this generalization. However, this claim for efficiency by the older learner can be made, whether we are talking about learning a second language or mathematics, geography or physics. There is also very strong support in favour of the position that the more time spent studying a second language, the greater the probability that the individual will achieve a high level of sophistication in the language. This issue is discussed in greater detail by Genesee (Chapter 3) in relation to research findings on early versus late immersion programs in Canada.

What then are the implications of recognizing that there are advantages to second language teaching at an early age, despite the fact the young child is not the most efficient learner of a second language? It is clear that the higher the level of achievement desired, the earlier one should begin, the more time should be spent, and the more opportunity there should be for using the language in real acts of communication. The danger is that if the program itself is not appropriate, students will turn away from learning a second language at an early point in their education. A poor language program will counterproductively create undesired attitudes and values, and at the moment there is sufficient information available to suggest that this is happening, in general, with core French programs. This negative emphasis is not happening with the more extensive programs such as extended and immersion. Immersion, in fact, has been very successful (see Genesee, Chapter 3). Among the reasons for its success may be that a very early start leads to a basic grounding in the language, which then allows the language to be used in a practical way for further school subjects. The subject matter itself at the early grades is relatively simple and conceptually easier than in the later grades and therefore learning can begin with a far simpler vocabulary.

A final point is that, as is typically the case in answers to complex questions, there really is no optimal age (see Stern, 1978). If it is intended that a high proficiency level should be achieved, then there is an advantage to starting early. The early start has the advantage of providing more time in which learning can take place and secondly, it is an opportunity to avoid the negative motivational consequences that may accompany a start in the adolescent years.

Second language teaching programs for whom?

We need to consider which approach to French language teaching should be provided to different types of students. The types may be categorized as being either of a monitoring group engaging in language learning in order to acquire a language once possessed by their parents or grandparents, or members of the non-minority group who speak the majority language and wish to acquire a second language. The latter "majority group", have more choices because they can aspire to different levels of proficiency in the second language. The majority group may choose a level of achievement ranging from no second language learning, through a basic tourist level of achievement, and up to full language proficiency. For the majority group learner, there are real advantages to learning a second language but there is no necessity.

The minority group in general, however, does have both a necessary and a sufficient reason for learning a second language. The one exception is where the member of a minority group lives in a community of the minority language and does not anticipate leaving that community. At least 60% of Francophones in Quebec presumably put themselves into this category for they are unilingually French. But, when the minority group is submerged in the majority language, they not only must learn the majority language, but it is expected that they will learn it to a very high proficiency level. Parenthetically of course, one might note that even members of the minority group living in minority language communities may at some point wish to be tourists in the majority community and a survival knowledge of the dominant language may be useful.

This question "For Whom?" also raises the question of whether there are selection criteria by which to decide whether or not a given person should undertake the learning of a second language. There is evidence to show that reliable selection criteria do not now exist. There are studies which indicate, for example, that immersion programs, the most extensive of those available, are in fact suitable for all children (e.g. Genesee, Chapter 3). Studies have consistently shown that although intelligence, as measured by a standard IQ test, is related to the development of reading and writing skills in the second language, intelligence is unrelated to the development of speaking skills. In other words, children of relatively low IQ develop as much fluency in French as high IQ children (see Genesee, Chapter 3). Although this finding might at first appear surprising, it makes sense when one realizes that the immersion experience is designed to mimic the process through which the child learns his first language. Except in the case of certain severely retarded or autistic children, virtually all children learn to communicate in their first language irrespective of their level of intelligence. A second selection criterion which has been suggested is that of socioeconomic status. However, the evidence is clear that children from working class backgrounds are as capable as any of learning a second language (see Genesee, Chapter 3). It is also true that children who come from a minority (non-official) language home also do well in learning additional languages (see Cummins, Chapter 5). In fact, there is some evidence that children from certain linguistic backgrounds, such as Italian, may have an advantage in learning French because of the similarity between languages.

Motivation has been suggested as a selection criterion. It is likely that a high level of motivation for second language learning is probably a prerequisite in an immersion program that starts in the later grade levels. However, this does not mean that a high level of motivation is required in an early immersion program. One can assume high motivation much more readily at the kindergarten and grade one levels than one can in the junior high or intermediate levels. In addition, the relatively concrete nature of the curriculum at the younger age level provides children with a breather space in which to acquire sufficient French skills to master the academic content. At the higher levels, the students must be highly motivated to overcome the language barrier, and at the same time, to master the more complex curriculum content being presented through French.

It has been suggested that for certain children, it would be disadvantageous to teach a second language. The suggestion has been made that some children are more predisposed to develop learning disabilities in second language programs of the early immersion type than they would be in a regular English program (Trites, 1978). The evidence on this question is far from convincing, and there is equally good evidence on the other side to show that children who begin school with language disabilities do as well in early total immersion as do comparable children in regular programs, in addition to acquiring fluent French skills (see Bruck, 1978; Genesee, Chapter 3). However, similar language disabled children in regular programs experience considerable difficulty in core second language courses, and there have been some reasons which have been suggested as to why these learning disadvantaged children do better in early total immersion. Firstly, reading skills may be easier to acquire in French in view of the fact that the sound-symbol relationships are more systematic in French than in English; secondly, the language disabled child's self-esteem may be boosted by the fact that he is acquiring French skills, something that other siblings or peers may not have. Parenthetically, one may also note that this additional learning on the part of immersion children may also have a special advantage in that it is the only school learning provided in which the child may quickly discover that he has skills not possessed even by his parents. It is interesting to speculate as to what special advantages in the area of personality development this may provide for the immersion child.

Conclusions

Before concluding this discussion, a brief reference to the costs of second language teaching programs will be made. One must look at the costs of inclusion as well as of exclusion, and one must consider both financial and social costs of the program as they relate to students enroled in second language programs. Recently, there has been some important research in the area of costs (Churchill, 1978; MacNab & Unitt, 1978). The costs associated with core programs that use itinerant French teacher specialists are greater than the school program costs would have been had such specialist teaching not been included. This statement, of course, is not specific to second language teaching. It is also true that it costs more to provide physical education in the elementary schools via a specialist rather than the classroom teacher. The same kind of statement is not made at the high school level or any grade level where the curriculum is taught by specialists. But it is true at the elementary level. When one teacher is responsible for one classroom, the addition of a specialist means that the pupil-teacher ratio has been lowered. With respect to social costs, the learning of a second language is always positive. There are no known disadvantages of a social nature to acquiring a second language. The non-acquisition of the language — the exclusion of second language teaching — simply prevents the acquisition of these social benefits. In the most negative scenario, in a country such as Canada which is officially bilingual, the exclusion may have a direct negative cost in that it may prevent a proper appreciation of the fact that members of the other official group do have to learn the second language. They do not have the option of not acquiring both languages. The final cost may simply be the totally unmeasurable one of maintaining two solitudes.

In summary, one should reiterate the importance of matching aspiration level in second language teaching with the teaching approach. It is a serious mistake to allow people to believe that the core French teaching program will produce functional levels of proficiency in the second language. If it is intended that the language become available to the learner for social communication, if it is intended that the person acquire sufficient knowledge in a language to be able to operate comfortably in the second language environment, then core French is not the right program. If, on the other hand, all that is wanted is tourist French, then core French is appropriate.

The final point is to reiterate that second language programs can be very successful. And given that programs such as immersion can be successful at no important extra cost, one may wonder why they are not available for everyone. If we accept the premise that learning is a good thing, if we have clear evidence that additional learning is a good thing, and can be made available for very little additional cost (some would argue at no additional cost), then one really does have to wonder why everyone is not enroled in an effective second language teaching program. It is fairly clear that certain segments of Canadian society (as are segments of European society) are learning second languages. The more important question to pose is not

Why? Where? When? and For Whom? should second language teaching programs be provided, but rather, why are we now providing educational programs in such a way as to effectively exclude second language learning from the general population? The issue is less one of why an élite group is now benefiting from the effective forms of second language teaching, and more a question of why the non-élite members of society are not benefiting from such learning. In Canada at least, with two official languages, effective second language learning would offer one mechanism for removing the unnecessary distinctions that now occur in the graduates from our schools. If we truly believed in an egalitarian society, we would have very little choice but to provide school situations such that all children would have equal access to effective second language teaching programs.

References

BRUCK, M. 1978, The suitability of early French immersion programs for the language disabled child. *The Canadian Modern Language Review*, 34, 884–87.

BURSTALL, C., JAMIESON, M., COHEN, S. & HARGREAVES, M. 1974, *Primary French in the balance*. Windsor, England: National Foundation for Educational Research.

CARROLL, J. B. 1975, *The teaching of French as a foreign language in eight countries*. New York: John Wiley.

CHURCHILL, S. 1978, *Costs: French Language Instructional Units*. Toronto: Ontario Ministry of Education.

CZIKO, G. A., LAMBERT, W. E., SIDOTI, N. & TUCKER, F. R. 1980, Graduates of early immersion: Retrospective views of grade 11 students and their parents. In R. N. ST. CLAIR & H. GILES (eds), *The Social and psychological contents of language*. Hillsdale, N.J.: L. Erlbaum and Associates.

DESROCHERS, A. & CLEMENT, R. 1979, *The social psychology of inter-ethnic contact and cross-cultural communication: An annotated bibliography*. Quebec: Laval University, International Center for Research on Bilingualism.

ENGLE, P. 1975, Language medium in early school years for minority language groups. *Review of Educational Research*, 45, 283–325.

MACNAB, G. L. & UNITT, J. 1978, *A cost analysis model for programs in French as a second language*. Toronto: Ontario Ministry of Education.

OFFICIAL LANGUAGES ACT. 1969, Ottawa: Government of Canada.

ONTARIO MINISTRY OF EDUCATION. 1974, *Report of the Ministerial Committee on the teaching of French* (The Gillin Report). Toronto: Ontario Ministry of Education.

PEAL, E. & LAMBERT, W. E. 1967, The relation of bilingualism to intelligence. In J. MICHEL (ed.), *Foreign language teaching*. New York: Macmillan, 143–91.

PENFIELD, W. 1967, The learning of languages. In J. MICHEL (ed.), *Foreign language teaching*. New York: Macmillan, 192–214.

SECRETARY OF STATE. 1979, *Where to learn French or English/Ou apprendre l'anglais et le français*. Ottawa: Minister of Supply and Services.

SHAPSON, S. & PURBHOO, M. 1977, A transition program for Italian children. *The Canadian Modern Language Review*, 33, 486–96.

STERN, H. H. 1978, French immersion in Canada: Achievement and directions. *The Canadian Modern Language Review*, 34, 836–54.

SWAIN, M. 1981, Linguistic environment as a factor in the acquisition of target language skills. In R. ANDERSON (ed.), *Second language acquisition and use under difference circumstances*. Rowley, Mass.: Newbury House.

TORONTO BOARD OF EDUCATION. 1975, Report of the work group on multicultural programs. Toronto: The Board of Education for the City of Toronto.

TRITES, R. 1978, Learning disabilities in immersion. *The Canadian Modern Language Review*, 34, 888–89.

TUCKER, R. 1974, Methods of second language teaching. *The Canadian Modern Language Review*, 31, 102–107.

3 French immersion programs

Fred Genesee
McGill University

Abstract. A number of alternative French immersion programs are described with discussion focusing on early total immersion (ETI) and late immersion (LI) options. The results of extensive evaluations of the effectiveness of immersion programs are summarized. Implications of the results as they pertain to learner characteristics (including age and intellectual ability), program types, language sequencing, and follow-up programs are discussed.

The early 1960's were a turning point in the history of Quebec and perhaps of Canada. This period, which has come to be known as the Quiet Revolution, entailed radical redevelopments in the structures and values of French Canadian society in Quebec. Most notably, in education, it included the formation of a provincial Ministry of Education, and subsequently the creation of universal, and compulsory, elementary and secondary education, and the development of a province-wide system of junior colleges. Culturally, the Quiet Revolution was marked by the assurgence of the French language, which previously had occupied a position secondary to that of English despite the fact that 80% of the province's residents were French-speaking — many, in fact, spoke only French. French began to gain greater currency and much deserved legitimacy as a language of communication in all aspects of Quebec life, even in business, which had previously been completely dominated by the English language.

This situation had serious repercussions for the English community. In particular, there was concern about the effectiveness of French language instruction in the English schools. English-speaking parents became dissatisfied with the generally low level of competence their children were achieving in French, even after 12 years of schooling. Faced with the growing importance of the French language and the apparent ineffectiveness of existing instructional methods, Anglophone parents began to consider alternatives to the existing traditional or core method of second language instruction (see Halpern, Chapter 2). In their search, they solicited the opinions of local experts, such as Wilder Penfield of the Montreal Neurological Institute, who had established an international reputation for his work on the brain and language, and Wallace Lambert of McGill University, who had also established a considerable reputation internationally for his work on the social psychology of bilingualism. Together they formed a team from which the French immersion programs evolved. This model of teamwork, involving as it did parents, educators, researchers and other specialists, had continued to characterize the development of immersion programs across Canada. There are few social issues which can boast such excellent voluntary co-operation (see Lambert & Tucker, 1972, for a review of the origins of French immersion).

Immersion program descriptions

Early immersion

The French immersion program that initially evolved was *early total immersion* (ETI) and was designed to: (a) capitalize on children's apparent ability to learn language incidentally and apparently effortlessly; (b) take advantage of their social naïveté and attitudinal openness; (c) reflect the same processes that characterize first language learning by emphasizing the use of language for communicative purposes; and (d) do all this without in any way retarding the participating children's native language development, academic achievement or general cognitive development.

During the first three years of the ETI program (kindergarten to grade two), all classroom instruction is presented exclusively in French by teachers with native or native-like competence in French. Thus, the children are taught to read, write, spell and do mathematics in French, their second language, before they are taught these skills in English. During kindergarten and the first few months of grade one, emphasis is placed on developing listening comprehension skills in French. By December of grade one, students in most classes are encouraged to speak French in the classroom. The teachers are instructed to use French at all times with the pupils, except during emergencies, despite the fact that initially the children speak English amongst themselves and even with the teacher. The teachers are also instructed not to over-correct the children's errors when they begin to speak French. This strategy is adopted in order to eliminate the frustrations and inhibitions that can result if learners are repeatedly corrected for making mistakes in their early use of the second language. Grammar and vocabulary are dealt with in the French language arts period.

Instruction in the English language is introduced into the immersion curriculum in either grade two (Lambert & Tucker, 1972) grade three (Genesee, 1978a) or, in some cases, as late as grade four or five (Genesee & Lambert, 1983; Gray, 1981). Initially, English is used to teach English language arts for approximately one hour a day or 20% of daily instructional time. Instructional time in English is increased in subsequent grades by teaching regular subjects, such as mathematics, through English. The rate of increase of English instruction varies from program to program. It increases quickly in most Montreal programs (i.e. grade two = 20%, grade three = 30%, grade four = 40%, grades five and six = 60%) but much more slowly in some Ottawa programs (i.e. grades two to five = 20%; grade six = 50%; see Morrison, 1981). The implications of these instructional time variations for first and second language achievement will be discussed later.

At the secondary school level the ETI students are offered a "follow-up program" consisting of certain course options intended to maintain and enhance their second language skills. These courses are not necessarily language courses, but may be regular content courses, such as history, geography, or mathematics. The students can choose up to 40% of their courses at the secondary level in French.

To recapitulate, there are three phases to the ETI program: an *immersion phase*, from kindergarten to grade two, when French is used as the sole medium of instruction; a *bilingual phase*, from grade three to the end of elementary school, when both English and French are used, in varying proportions, as media of instruction; a *maintenance phase*, at the secondary level, when select courses are taught in French. The last two phases constitute what is referred to as the follow-up to the ETI program.

Late immersion

Since inauguration of the ETI program, alternative forms of immersion have been developed, most notably late immersion (LI). LI programs postpone use of French as the main medium of instruction until the end of elementary school or the beginning of secondary school (e.g. grades seven or eight). There are typically two types of LI, a one-year and a two-year option. In *one-year* LI programs, all curriculum instruction, or most, with the exception of English language arts, is taught through French for one year (e.g. Genesee, Polich & Stanley, 1977; Swain, 1978). In *two-year* LI programs, this schedule is repeated for two consecutive years (e.g. Genesee, 1981a; Morrison, 1981). LI programs may be preceded by traditional or core French second language (FSL) instruction during the elementary grades (Genesee, Polich & Stanley, 1977; Halpern, Chapter 2) or they may be preceded by special preparatory second language courses one or two years immediately prior to immersion (Swain, 1978). The follow-up program for most LI options in the higher grades have comprised advanced second language arts courses and, in some cases, selected optional non-language courses, such as history, which are taught through French.

An additional variant of the LI alternative involves the setting of the program. Most LI programs are located in high schools which also offer the regular English program. In these cases the immersion classes are often situated in a separate "wing" of the school in order to create a French ambience; the language of the school is otherwise English. Some LI programs, however, are housed in "centres" which offer only LI; in these cases all communication in the school is conducted in French. A similar distinction can also be found in the case of ETI programs.

The curriculum in a LI program is the same as that in a regular English program; the students are expected to cover the same academic material during the course of the year despite the fact that all academic instruction is given in French. A transition period during the first couple of months is required in order to provide the students with the language skills they require for effective learning of subject matter. This transition is usually achieved easily and quickly in the case of LI preceded by a core French program from kindergarten, but tends to be longer and is less effective if the students have only had "preparatory" French courses immediately prior to immersion.

Evaluation studies of immersion programs

Numerous long-term evaluation studies have been conducted to assess the impact of the various immersion programs. This research has addressed three general issues:

(a) the effect of participation in immersion programs on the students' English language development;
(b) the effect of receiving instruction through a second language on academic achievement;
(c) the effectiveness of immersion programs in promoting second language proficiency.

The suitability of immersion programs for students with special linguistic, intellectual, and socio-economic characteristics has also been investigated by some researchers, and these findings will be reviewed as well.

First, a few words concerning evaluation procedures. In general, the linguistic and academic outcomes of the programs have been assessed by comparing the performance of immersion students to that of carefully selected comparison groups of students on a variety of tests. Two types of comparison groups have been used: (a) English comparison groups (EC) consisting of English-speaking students attending regular English programs; and (b) French comparison groups (FC) consisting of French-speaking students attending regular French schools. Students in all groups have been equated on age, intellectual ability, and, as much as possible, on socio-economic indices.

A variety of tests have been used during the evaluations to measure different types of English language, French language, and academic skills at different grade levels. Many of the English language tests that have been used are commercially-available standardized tests, such as the Metropolitan and California Achievement Tests, which assess: word knowledge, vocabulary, spelling, punctuation, capitalization and grammar. Other tests, such as speaking, listening comprehension, and writing tests, have been developed by the researchers. The French language tests have usually been French-mother tongue tests; they were designed for use with native French-speaking students and tend to reflect features of Canadian or Quebec culture. Existing French tests have been used when available and appropriate; otherwise, they were developed by the researchers. Two types of academic achievement tests have been used: commercially-available, standardized tests (e.g., mathematics); and in some cases the secondary school leaving Examinations set by the Quebec Ministry of Education.

Early immersion results

English language development. The results of English language testing prior to the introduction of English instruction has indicated that ETI students generally scored lower than the EC students on tests which required literacy skills in English: reading, word discrimination, spelling, and sight vocabulary. There have been relatively few significant differences between the ETI and EC students on tests not requiring literacy skills; listening comprehension, aural decoding, speaking skills, and oral vocabulary. Differences that have been found in the latter category tend to favour the immersion students. For example, Genesee, Tucker & Lambert (1975) found that ETI students were more sensitive communicators than EC students in face to face encounters, possibly because the former have experienced communication difficulties in the immersion program and have learned to detect and respond better to the communicative demands of a situation. The findings of a deficit in English literacy skills is not surprising in view of the ETI students' lack of formal training in these skills. More surprising has been the finding that the immersion students are able to complete and score reasonably well on the English tests prior to receiving any instruction in English. It seems likely that this ís possible because of the transfer to English of language arts skills acquired in French.

Testing at the end of one year after English language arts is introduced has indicated that the ETI students have achieved parity with EC students on all English language tests with the exception of spelling where the immersion students tend to lag. Testing at the end of grades four to six indicated that the immersion students continue to perform as well as the EC students in all areas under assessment, including writing (Genesee & Stanley, 1976). The lag in acquisition of English spelling patterns among the immersion students is usually redressed by the end of grade five.

Comparisons have also been made among above-average, average, and below-average students, as defined by IQ scores. Genesee (1978a) found that the below-average students in the immersion program scored at the same level as their below-average peers in the English program. In other words, the performance of below-average students who had not received any English language arts instruction until grade three were not handicapped in any way in their English language development.

Thus, there has been no evidence of long-term deficits in the English language development of the immersion students. These findings have been found consistently in Quebec (Genesee, 1978a; Lambert & Tucker, 1972), in Ontario (Stern, Swain & McLean, 1976), in New Brunswick (Gray, 1981), and in British Columbia (Shapson & Day, 1982).

Evaluations of alternative ETI programs in which English instruction is introduced in grade two, three or four have revealed no advantage to English language proficiency as a result of introducing English into the curriculum earlier, in grade two, or later, in grade four. Conversely English language development does not suffer as a result of delaying English instruction. This is true even in the case of double immersion, or trilingual programs, where two second languages are used as the sole medium of instruction for approximately half of the school day each until English is introduced in grade four (Genesee & Lambert, 1983).

Academic achievement. The results of mathematics testing in grades one to six revealed that even at the primary grade levels, ETI students acquire competence in most aspects of mathematics that is as good as that of EC students despite the fact that the former group had received mathematics instruction via a second language. The one exception to this finding is in the area of problem solving which requires competence in English reading. In this case, it has been found that ETI students sometimes lag behind the EC students until they have been taught to read English. Swain (1978) reports that students in early immersion programs of the Ottawa/Carleton Board of Education also performed as well as English comparison students on achievement tests in science.

As in the case of English language skills, it was found that the mathematics performance of below-average students in the EI program was comparable to that of below-average students in the EC program, albeit poorer than that of average and above-average students. Thus, again there was no indication that below-average students were handicapped by the immersion experience. Thus, in general, these results indicate that ETI students learn content material as well as EC students despite the fact that instruction in these subjects is provided in a second language.

French language skills. The performance of the ETI students has been found to be vastly superior to that of the EC students on all French language tests, including reading, grammar, spelling, listening comprehension, and speaking. In comparison to the performance of native French-speaking students of the same age, the pattern of results is somewhat more complex. The immersion students' performance has been found to be most comparable to that of French-speaking students on tests which assess the ability to decode French, such as listening comprehension and reading comprehension. The performance of immersion students on tests which assessed productive skills, such as speaking, has been found to be less than native-like, although very good. For example, the speaking skills of Montreal ETI students during a personal interview in French was rated by native French-speaking Canadians to be poorer than those of native French speakers, but in the "high range" (3 to 5 on a 5 point scale, with 5 representing native-like or excellent competence). ETI students can converse freely and creatively on diverse topics in French and are relatively undaunted by gaps in their knowledge of French grammar or vocabulary.

Genesee (1976a) has analyzed the French test results according to the students' IQ level, and has found that the acquisition of literacy skills in French, such as reading, is associated with IQ level so that above-average students score higher on reading tests than average or below-average students. This relationship is quite typical of literacy skills. On the other hand, the acquisition of interpersonal communication skills in French, such as, listening comprehension and speaking, was not found to be associated with IQ level; below-average students were rated as highly as the above-average students on these latter skills. It would appear from these results that students representing a wide range of academic ability levels may be equally able to acquire second language listening comprehension and speaking skills.

Some alternatives to ETI have evolved that increase exposure to English while concomitantly reducing exposure to French. A number of school districts offer *partial* immersion programs in which approximately 50% of instruction time is spent in French and 50% in English beginning in grade one. There is no evidence from evaluations of partial immersion programs that this reduced use of French as a medium of instruction during the primary grades yields greater proficiency in English language skills than that achieved in an early total immersion program. At the same time, however, it has been found that reduction in the use of French as a language of instruction in a partial immersion program *reduces* the level of second language proficiency of participating students relative to that of early immersion students (Genesee, 1981b; Swain, 1978).

In summary, the results of the French language testing of ETI students indicate that: (a) the immersion students acquire "native-like" or near native-like proficiency in decoding French; (b) they acquire very good although not native-like functional oral communication skills in French; (c) acquisition of literacy skills in French is associated with the students' IQ level whereas acquisition of interpersonal communication skills is not; and (d) reduction in the use of French as a language of instruction appears to decrease the second language proficiency of participating students.

Late immersion results

English language development. There has been no evidence that the English skills of students participating in *one-year* late immersion programs beginning in grade seven have suffered (Genesee, Polich & Stanley, 1977). In fact, where differences have been found between LI and EC students, they favour the immersion group despite statistical controls on intelligence. Moreover, as in the case of ETI, there has been no evidence that below-average students in LI are handicapped in English language development as a result of the immersion experience; their language skills develop to the same level as those of below-average students in the regular English program.

Academic achievement. The academic achievement of one-year LI students has not been found to be impeded by the use of a second language for course instruction. This is attested to by the results of standardized achievement tests in mathematics and by the results of graduating students on secondary school Leaving Examinations set by the Quebec Ministry of Education (Genesee & Chaplin, 1976; Genesee, 1977).

In the case of standardized testing in mathematics, it has been found that the LI students score at the same level as EC students despite the fact that the former students receive mathematics instruction for at least one year in French. Furthermore, there has been no indication of significant differences between the performance of the below-average LI students and that of below-average EC students (Genesee, Polich & Stanley, 1977). In other words, the below-average students in LI were not handicapped in mathematics by instruction through French.

In the case of results from Departmental Leaving Examinations, Genesee (1977) has compared the performance of one-year late immersion students who wrote examinations in French, such as chemistry and mathematics, with (a) the performance of other English students who wrote the equivalent examinations in English; and (b) norms based on native French-speaking secondary school students throughout Quebec. The results revealed that, even after the influence of IQ had been statistically controlled, students from the LI program scored at least as well as their peers in the EC program on examinations of English language skills, physics, chemistry and history. With respect to provincial norms based on native French-speaking students, it was found that the LI students scored higher on the average than their Francophone peers in the rest of Quebec who wrote the same examinations; these examinations included *histoire, géographie, mathématiques, dactylo,* and *arts plastiques.* Interpretation of these results must be made cautiously to take into account various socio-economic, demographic and academic factors. In particular, the students comprising the LI samples were probably different from the provincial norming group in that they were from socio-economically relatively advantaged families; and they were probably academically stronger owing to the effect of student selection factors in immersion programs.

French language skills. The results of French language testing in *one-year* LI programs revealed the same basic pattern as that found in the ETI program. That is, one-year LI students achieve native-like or near native-like competence in decoding skills, such as listening and reading comprehension, but less than native-like but very good competence in production skills, such as speaking. The LI students acquire significantly higher levels of proficiency in all aspects of French than do comparable EC students.

Evidence concerning the relationship between IQ level and French competence has been less clear-cut in the case of the LI program. In particular, intelligence seemed to play a more important role in the acquisition of all types of second language skills at the secondary school level than was found to be the case at the elementary level. Genesee & Chaplin (1976) found that grade eleven above-average LI students tend to outperform average students on tests of speaking and listening comprehension. Whether this is due to programmatic factors or a difference in the language learning style of LI versus ETI students is not clear. Genesee also found that intelligence played a significant role in the acquisition of literacy skills in French (as in English) among LI students as was found for ETI students.

Two-year late immersion results. As has been noted in the case of ETI and one-year LI evaluations, there has been no evidence in the case of the *two-year* LI option that the participating students suffer any setbacks to English language development or academic achievement. At the same time, they acquire significantly higher levels of proficiency in French than do students who have been following the regular English program with core FSL instruction (Adiv & Morcos, 1979; Genesee & Leblanc, 1978; and Genesee & Morcos, 1978). Evaluations of the two-year LI program have focused on the relative effectiveness of this option versus the one-year alternative and versus the early total immersion program.

Early versus late immersion results

Comparisons between the ETI program and the *one-year* LI alternative have indicated that ETI students generally achieve higher levels of proficiency in French than do LI students (Cziko, Holobow & Lambert, 1977; Genesee, 1981a; Lapkin, Swain, Kamin & Hanna, 1983). This finding is based on tests of reading, listening comprehension, oral production, grammar, and writing, and has been found for LI preceded by core FSL from kindergarten (Genesee, 1981a) and for LI preceded by preparatory FSL instruction only (Swain, 1978).

Two sets of studies have compared ETI with *two-year* LI, those carried out in Montreal (Adiv & Morcos, 1979; Genesee, 1981a) and those in Ottawa (Morrison, 1981). The Montreal studies assessed the French proficiency of ETI and two-year (grades seven and eight) LI students over four consecutive years until the end of grade eleven. They consistently failed to find significant differences between samples of students drawn from these types of program on measures which included listening comprehension, oral production, reading comprehension, dictation, and writing tests. In contrast, Morrison (1981) has consistently found statistically significant differences in favour of students who had been in an ETI program in comparison with students from a two-year (grades seven and eight) LI program.

Comparison of the Montreal and Ottawa programs reveals one likely basis for this apparent inconsistency. The Ottawa ETI program provides much more French during the follow-up phases than does the Montreal program while the LI programs in both cities are quite comparable. Thus, one possible explanation for the advantage of the Ottawa ETI program lies in the additional exposure to French that it provides relative to the Montreal program. Indeed, the results of a number of other evaluations, such as those referred to earlier involving partial immersion (Genesee, 1981b; Swain, 1978) suggest that amount of exposure to French may be an important factor in determining level of second language achievement. The importance of in-school exposure to the second language is underlined by surveys carried out with grade six and eleven immersion and non-immersion students (Genesee, 1978b; 1981c). Immersion students in Montreal reported that they were not making significantly greater use of French outside school than were non-immersion students, except in interpersonal encounters. Swain (1981) has come to a similar conclusion after comparing the French language proficiency of students in immersion programs located in cities across Canada. She found that there were no appreciable differences in the French competence of students in cities with a high percentage of French-speaking residents compared to cities with a low percentage of French speakers.

An additional factor that may also account, in part at least, for the Montreal–Ottawa discrepancy is the nature of the programs themselves. Informal observations of the two programs indicate that the Ottawa ETI program uses a more individualized, activity-based approach whereas the Montreal programs are generally group-oriented and teacher-centred (Obadia, personal communication, 1978). Although there is a lack of formal, systematic evidence to validate this characterization of these programs, Stevens (1976) obtained some empirical evidence indicating that an individualized, activity-based approach to immersion can be very effective when implemented systematically relative to a more conventional group-oriented, teacher-centred approach.

To the extent that some of the pedagogical differences examined by Stevens (1976) are also reflected in the Ottawa and Montreal programs, they may provide an additional explanation, along with the time factor, for the achievement differences reported in the evaluations from Montreal and Ottawa. In any event, Stevens' findings illustrate that programmatic factors can have a substantial impact on second language learning in immersion programs, and more specifically, that activity-based, student-centred approaches may be particularly effective in second language learning programs. To date, there is a lack of systematic descriptive information concerning the actual pedagogical procedures used by immersion teachers. Thus, for example, there is no clear picture of the nature of teacher-student interactions, teachers' methods of correcting pupil errors, or the integration of language arts courses with the learner's actual linguistic needs. These lacunae offer a rich basis for further research on immersion.

Notwithstanding programmatic factors, the findings that the two-year LI students in Montreal achieved parity with the ETI students despite the latter's greater cumulative exposure to French at the time of evaluation attest to the greater learning efficiency of older students. Similar findings have been reported by other researchers (Asher & Price, 1967; Burstall *et al.*, 1974; Fathman, 1975; Price, 1978; Stern, 1963). Thus, an advantage to starting second language instruction late appears to be the apparent efficiency of the learning process characteristic of the older student. At the same time, the Ottawa results indicate that there is an advantage associated with early second language instruction. Instruction beginning in kindergarten, as it does in early immersion, makes available 12 to 13 years of schooling during which second language learning can take place. This contrasts with the 5 to 7 years that are available if second language instruction begins in grade seven or eight, as is customary for most late immersion programs. A corollary advantage associated with extended second language exposure in school is the opportunity for extended use of the language outside school. Needless to say, extracurricular use is also available to older students as well, but their shortened program will reduce their extracurricular opportunities commensurately. The possibility of extracurricular use of the second language and, thereby, of extending and enhancing linguistic competence should be a major consideration in bilingual communities where real possibilities to use the language exist. This type of exposure is likely to be particularly important since it has been found that individuals who begin second language learning in childhood in natural settings generally achieve higher levels of proficiency in the long term than those who begin in adolescence or adulthood (Asher & Garcia, 1969; Oyama, 1976; Seliger, Krashen & Ladefoged, 1975).

The suitability of immersion for all students

The well documented success of the first immersion programs in Quebec was accompanied by a rather dramatic increase in demand among parents to make immersion available to their children. Concern was often expressed, however, that immersion might not be suitable for all children. The added challenge of dealing with a second language in addition to regular school work was thought to constitute an insurmountable obstacle with detrimental academic, linguistic, and cognitive effects for some children. In response to those concerns a number of empirical investigations have been carried out to systematically assess the success, or failure, of students who might be expected to do more poorly in immersion than in the regular

English program. Students with the following characteristics have been investigated: (a) students with below-average academic ability; (b) children with language or learning disabilities; and (c) children from lower socio-economic backgrounds. Findings from these investigations and the question of immersion programs for minority language children are now reviewed.

Academic ability and success in immersion

As has already been noted, Genesee (1976a) examined the importance of general academic ability for success in both ETI and one-year LI programs. Academic ability was defined in terms of the students' score on a group administered IQ test (Lorge-Thorndike, 1967). Students in grades four to six of an ETI program and in grades seven to eleven of a one-year LI program were classified as average (IQ score between 96 and 115), above-average (IQ score above 115) and below-average (score below 96) and their performance on a battery of English language, French language, and mathematics tests was subsequently compared to that of students in the regular English program who had been similarly classified.

Briefly, as expected the below-average students in both immersion and non-immersion programs scored significantly lower than the corresponding average students on most of the tests, and likewise the average students scored lower than the above-average students. Below-average students in the immersion programs, early and late, did not score significantly differently than the below-average students in the regular English program on tests of English language achievement (including reading, spelling, vocabulary, writing) or mathematics. Thus, the below-average students in immersion were not differentially handicapped in their first language development and academic achievement as a result of being in immersion.

At the same time, the below-average students in immersion scored significantly higher than their below-average counterparts in the core FSL program on all of the French language tests (including listening comprehension, speaking, reading and grammar) attesting to their ability to benefit from the immersion experience.

Comparisons of the French test results of the ability subgroups in the immersion samples themselves revealed some interesting findings. Below-average ETI students were found to score significantly lower than average and above-average ETI students on tests assessing French language skills that are literacy-based (e.g. reading and spelling). In contrast, however, the below-average ETI students scored at the same level as the average and above-average immersion subgroups on tests which assessed interpersonal communication skills in French (i.e. speaking and listening comprehension; Genesee, 1976a).

The differential relationship between IQ and type of French language proficiency was consistently characteristic of the performance of ETI samples evaluated in grades four to six. While this pattern was also evident in the case of the one-year LI students at certain grade levels, it was much less consistent. In particular, there was a statistically significant tendency for level of IQ and level of interpersonal communication skills in French to be positively associated in the LI program. Tucker, Hamayan & Genesee (1976) reported similar differential effects for IQ in a study that assessed the relationship between multiple factors and the French language achievement of ETI and LI students. They found that a predictor factor that included performance on an IQ test was more important for predicting achievement in listening comprehension and oral production in the case of LI than in the case of ETI students.

The lack of significant differences that characterized the performance of the IQ subgroups in the ETI program on tests of interpersonal communication skills in French is consistent with the findings of other researchers who have also found that IQ is not the exclusive or necessarily the most important correlate of second language achievement (Dockrell & Brosseau, 1967; Gardner & Lambert, 1972; Malherbe, 1946). These findings are also compatible with what we know about first language acquisition, namely, that all children, with a few pathological exceptions, acquire oral/aural competence in their native language. It follows, therefore, that second language programs designed to develop the learners' interpersonal communicative competence are likely to be more successful with a broad range of students than programs oriented towards literacy-based proficiency. The latter type of program is likely to produce the performance hierarchies that are traditional in academic programs. Another possibility is that the second language learning strategies used by older students are different than those used by younger students. In this regard, Krashen's (1981) notion of high monitor users who rely on the conscious manipulation of linguistic rules may be relevant; older learners may make greater use of conscious intellectual strategies to learn second language skills, even those that might otherwise be best learned using the unconscious strategies characteristic of first language acquisition.

Language/learning disabled children in immersion

Two independent series of investigations on the suitability of early immersion programs for language/learning disabled children have been carried out with conflicting findings and opposing implications (Bruck, 1978; Trites, 1981). To date, similar research has not been undertaken in the context of LI.

In Bruck's research, children in ETI programs who were classified as having a language/learning disability were matched with comparably disabled children in the regular English program. All children so classified had normal levels of intelligence. They were identified in kindergarten and they were assessed each year until the end of grade three, on a battery of English language, French language, and arithmetic tests. The performance of the two disabled groups was also compared to that of control groups who were identified in the immersion and English programs as not having language/learning disabilities. The results at the end of grade three indicated that it took the disabled children in both programs longer to attain basic literacy and academic skills than their non-disabled peers, as would be expected from their disability, but the disabled children in the immersion program had developed linguistic, cognitive and academic skills at a rate similar to that which would develop in a regular English classroom (Bruck, 1978). At the same time, the disabled immersion students showed good progress in French language learning. Bruck concluded that:

"children with language disabilities can benefit from and learn in French immersion programs . . . they should not be excluded from such programs merely because it is felt that their first language development is poor." (1978: 70)

Trites (1981), on the other hand, contends that there is a distinct subgroup of children who cannot make satisfactory progress in early immersion programs because they have a unique difficulty associated with a maturational lag in the development of temporal lobe regions of the brain. The putative source of their difficulty in immersion, according to Trites, is evidenced in their performance on a Tactual Performance Task. Trites recommends that these children be held back from immersion programs until higher grade levels, at which age their developmental lag would be breached. Trites contends further that it is possible to identify these children in pre-school before they encounter any difficulties.

Although based on a series of well designed, longitudinal studies involving a large number of test instruments and control groups, Trites' interpretations of his results are open to question (see also Canadian Modern Language Review, 1976). For example, Trites' evidence of a unique difficulty profile is based on the performance of ETI students who were referred to the Neuropsychology Laboratory of the Royal Ottawa Hospital because of difficulties they were encountering in the program. It is not strictly valid to conclude, as Trites does, that the test performance of this subgroup of referrals constitutes a valid predictor of difficulty in immersion without examining the performance of a sample of students who remain in the program.

Moreover, Trites' suggestion that children who evidence the putative maturational lag be held back from French immersion until later grades is questionable. This advice would be valid were it shown that it is specific to performance in an immersion program and not in an English program as well. There is no evidence in his studies to indicate that this is in fact the case. To the contrary, one would be quite surprised if the immersion "drop-outs" did not also have difficulties in the English program in view of Trites' own finding that these children scored very poorly on a battery of pretest measures, many of which are used customarily to determine readiness for schooling.

To summarize, it is not possible to conclude whether the difficulties experienced by the drop-outs examined by Trites are uniquely characteristic of children experiencing difficulty in immersion, and whether the same difficulties might not characterize these students' performance even in a regular English program. As Bruck's (1978) research illustrates, children who remain in immersion but who might otherwise be diagnosed as language/learning disabled and, therefore, poor candidates for immersion, can nevertheless benefit from this experience. If Trites' screening procedures were used, many children who might similarly benefit from an immersion program could be falsely excluded from participating in it.

Socio-economic factors and success in immersion

The majority of immersion programs in Canada are populated by children from middle to upper-middle class families and, consequently, the research findings are based on similarly constituted student samples. The suitability of immersion programs for children from lower socio-economic backgrounds has been addressed in three studies carried out in grades one and two in the Montreal area (Bruck, Tucker & Jakimik, 1975; Cziko, 1975; Tucker, Lambert & d'Anglejan, 1972). In these studies, the performance of ETI students from lower socio-economic backgrounds was compared to that of comparable children in the regular English program using a battery of English language and mathematics tests, and to that of French control children from working class backgrounds in a French school using a battery of French language tests.

It was found that in most cases the ETI pupils scored as well as the EC pupils on the English language tests; there were some tests on which the immersion group scored lower. As indicated earlier, this is quite typical of immersion prior to the introduction of English language arts instruction. There was no indication that the immersion students were having difficulty in mathematics relative to the EC groups. In the area of French language learning, it was found, as in the case of other evaluations, that the immersion students scored as well as the FC students on some of the tests, such as listening comprehension. In the Cziko study, it was also found that the lower socio-economic students in immersion scored as well as a control group comprised of middle-class immersion students on the French language tests. The children examined by Cziko were enroled in the same classes suggesting that the performance of his low socio-economic group may not be representative of all such children.

In sum, the extant research evidence indicates that children from lower socio-economic backgrounds can benefit from participation in an ETI program without apparent risk of native language deficits or academic difficulties. These findings are consistent with those previously reviewed for academically and linguistically disadvantaged children in demonstrating that students who might otherwise tend to do relatively poorly in school are not differentially handicapped in an immersion program. Additional research is needed, however, to assess the long term consequences of participation in ETI for these children and to evaluate the suitability of LI options for children from lower socio-economic backgrounds.

Minority language children and immersion

In contrast to the documented success of majority language children in second language immersion programs, members of minority language groups often experience disproportionately high rates of failure in schools where the majority language is used as the sole medium of instruction — so called "submersion" programs. Lambert (1980) has suggested that the success of many minority language children is often impeded in conventional public schools by the social denigration and threat of loss of the home language and culture that these children often experience. According to Cummins (Chapters 4, 5), minority language children often do poorly in school also because they do not acquire the communication skills in either their first language or the majority language that are necessary for school-based learning; thus, the mismatch between minority children's language skills and those demanded in the school setting contribute to these children's difficulties in school. Bruck's (1978) findings, already discussed, that even language disabled children from the majority language group can benefit from immersion, suggest that linguistic factors alone may be insufficient to account for the minority language children's general lack of success in school. Whatever the precise bases of these children's difficulties, one of the approaches suggested (see Cummins, Chapter 5) is that, contrary to the immersion formula, minority language children be educated mainly through their first language during the elementary years until such time as they can benefit fully from academic instruction in the majority language.

Notwithstanding the need for more empirical evidence on the suitability of immersion for minority language children (Genesee, 1976b), the socio-educational conditions that characterize and, therefore, possibly account for the success of immersion programs for majority language speakers are known and should be considered seriously by those who advocate "immersion" education for minority language children. Some of these conditions are: (a) respect for and use of the child's home language during the daily functioning of the school; (b) use of the child's home language to teach curriculum material; (c) an initial period during which the students are permitted to use their home language with one another and the teacher even though she/he addresses all comments in the child's second language; and (d) an emphasis on the child's communicative use of the second language and not on correct grammatical usage. Thus, immersion is not only a question of when and how much one teaches the students' first and second languages; it is more importantly a set of social conditions and educational approaches that facilitate learning. To create these conditions and methods to facilitate academic and language learning among minority language children may require changing the basic structure of immersion as it is known to apply to majority language children (e.g. San Diego City Schools, 1982).

Conclusions

By way of summarizing these studies, the following conclusions can be made with respect to English language development and academic achievement of students who participate in immersion programs:

1. There are no long-term deficits in English language development or academic achievement among students participating in early or late French immersion programs.

2. There does not appear to be any advantage to English language development from delaying or reducing the use of French as a medium of instruction.

3. Below-average students in either early or late immersion are not handicapped in native-language development or academic achievement by

instruction in a second language relative to their below-average peers in the regular English program.

4. Similarly, children with language disabilities or from lower socio-economic backgrounds who are in immersion programs have been found to progress at a normal rate in their first language and in academic areas when compared to comparable children educated through their first language.

With respect to French language skills, the following conclusions seem warranted:

1. Participation in an immersion program provides the student with greater competence in the French language than is usually achieved by students in traditional or core FSL programs.

2. Immersion students are more likely to achieve native-like or near native-like competence in decoding (or receptive) French skills than in encoding (or productive) French skills.

3. Delaying or reducing the use of French as a medium of instruction appears to yield lower levels of competence in French.

4. Below-average students in ETI appear to be able to acquire functional competence in speaking and understanding French to the same extent as average and above-average students in the program. However, intelligence seems to play a more important role in the acquisition of these skills in the case of late immersion — more intelligent students in the LI program tend to score higher on listening comprehension tests and to be rated higher on speaking skills than less intelligent students. It may be that the cognitive processes used by older second language learners are different than those used by younger learners. Further discussion and theories regarding the effects of bilingualism on academic functioning are provided by Cummins (Chapter 4).

5. Immersion programs have been shown to be effective in promoting second language proficiency among children with learning disabilities and among children from lower socio-economic backgrounds.

Since their inception in Quebec in 1965 immersion programs have been instituted across Canada and are presently available in a number of different languages, including Hebrew (Genesee & Lambert, 1983) and Ukrainian (Lupul, 1976) as well as French. In each case, the results of systematic, longitudinal studies continue to show that immersion programs are feasible and effective ways of providing predominantly majority English-speaking Canadian children with functional competence in French, their second language.

References

ADIV, E. & MORCOS, C. 1979, A comparison of three alternative French immersion programs at the grade 9 level. Montreal: The Protestant School Board of Greater Montreal, Instructional Services. November.

ASHER, J. & GARCIA, R. 1969, The optimal age to learn a foreign language. *Modern Language Journal*, 8, 334–41.

ASHER, J. J. & PRICE, B. S. 1967, The learning strategy of the total physical response: Some age differences. *Child Development*, 38, 1219–1227.

BRUCK, M. 1978, The suitability of early French immersion programs for the language-disabled child. *Canadian Journal of Education*, 3, 51–72.

BRUCK, M., TUCKER, G. R. & JAKIMIK, J. 1975, Are French immersion programs suitable for working class children? In W. VON RAFFLER ENGLE (ed.), *Prospects in child language*. The Hague: Mouton.

BURSTALL, C., JAMIESON, M., COHEN, S. & HARGREAVES, M. 1974, *Primary French in the balance*. Windsor, England: NFER Publishing Co.

THE CANADIAN MODERN LANGUAGE REVIEW 1976, Comments on guest analysts, 33, 208–15.

CZIKO, G. 1975, *The effects of different French immersion programs on the language and academic skills of children from various socioeconomic backgrounds*. M.A. thesis, Department of Psychology, McGill University.

CZIKO, G., HOLOBOW, N. & LAMBERT, W. E. 1977, *Early and late French immersion: A comparison of children at grade seven*. Department of Psychology, McGill University. April.

DOCKRELL, W. B. & BROSSEAU, J. F. 1967, The correlates of second language learning by young children. *Alberta Journal of Educational Research* 13, 295–98.

FATHMAN., A. 1975, The relationship between age and second language productive ability. *Language Learning*, 25, 245–53.

GARDNER, R. & LAMBERT, W. E. 1972, *Attitudes and motivation in second language learning*. Rowley, Mass.: Newbury House.

GENESEE, F. 1976a, The role of intelligence in second language learning. *Language Learning*, 26, 267–80.

— 1976b, The suitability of immersion programs for all children. *The Canadian Modern Language Review*, 32, 493–515.

— 1977, *Addendum to evaluation of the 1975–76 grade 11 French immersion class*. Montreal: The Protestant School Board of Greater Montreal, Instructional Services Department.

— 1978a, A longitudinal evaluation of an early immersion school program. *Canadian Journal of Education*, 3, 31–50.

— 1978b, Second language learning and language attitudes. *Working Papers on Bilingualism*, 19–42.

— 1981a, A comparison of early and late second language learning. *Canadian Journal of Behavioral Sciences*, 13, 115–27.

— 1981b, *Evaluation of the Laurenval early partial and early total immersion programs*. Psychology Department, McGill University. July.

— 1981c, Bilingualism and biliteracy: A study of cross-cultural contact in a bilingual community. In J. R. EDWARDS (ed.), *The social psychology of reading*. Silver Spring, Maryland: Institute of Modern Languages, 147–72.

GENESEE, F. & CHAPLIN, S. 1976, *Evaluation of the 1974–75 grade 11 French immersion class*. Psychology Department, Mcgill University.

GENESEE, F. & LAMBERT, W. E. 1983, Trilingual education for majority language children. *Child Development*, 54, 105–14.

GENESEE, F. & LEBLANC, M. 1978, *A comparative evaluation of three alternative French immersion programs: Grade 7 and 8*. Psychology Department, McGill University. January.

GENSEE, F. & MORCOS, C. 1978, *A comparative evaluation of three alternative French immersion programs: Grades 8 and 9*. Psychology Department, McGill University. December.

GENESEE, F., POLICH, E. & STANLEY, M. 1977, An experimental French immersion program at the secondary school level — 1969 to 1974. *The Canadian Modern Language Review*, 33, 318–32.

GENESEE, F. & STANLEY, M. 1976, The development of English writing skills in French immersion programs. *Canadian Journal of Education*, 3, 1–18.

GENESEE, F. TUCKER, G. R. & LAMBERT, W. E. 1975, Communication skills of bilingual children. *Child Development*, 46, 1010–1014.

GRAY, V. 1981, *Evaluation of the grade 6 French immersion program in Fredericton, New Brunswick*. Psychology Department, University of New Brunswick. February.

KRASHEN, S. D. 1981, Bilingual education and second language acquisition theory. *Schooling and language minority students: A theoretical framework*. Los Angeles, Calif.: Evaluation, Dissemination and Assessment Center, 51–79.

LAMBERT, W. E. 1980, The social psychology of language: A perspective for the 1980's. In H. GILES, W. P. ROBINSON & P. SMITH (eds), *Language: Social psychological perspectives*. Oxford: Pergamon Press, 415–24.

LAMBERT, W. E. & TUCKER, G. R. 1972, *The bilingual education of children: The St. Lambert experiment*. Rowley, Mass.: Newbury House.

LAPKIN, S., SWAIN, M., KAMIN, J. & HANNA, G. 1983, Late immersion in perspective: The Peel Study. *The Canadian Modern Language Review*, 39, 182–206.

LORGE-THORNDIKE. 1967, Intelligence Tests. Toronto: Nelson.

LUPUL, M. 1976, Bilingual education and the Ukrainians in western Canada: Possibilities and problems. In M. SWAIN (ed.), *Bilingualism in Canadian Education: Issues and Research*. Canadian Society for the Study of Education Yearbook, 3, 86–106.

MALHERBE, E. G. 1946, *The bilingual school*. London: Longmans, Green & Co.

MORRISON, F. 1981, *Evaluation of the second language learning (French) programs in Schools of the Ottawa and Carleton Boards of Education: Eighth annual report*. Ottawa: Ottawa Board of Education, Research Center.

OYAMA, S. 1976, A sensitive period for the acquisition of a non-native phonological system. *Journal of Psycholinguistic Research*, 5, 261–85.

PRICE, E. 1978, *Bilingual education in Wales: 5–11*. London: Evans/Methuen Educational.

SAN DIEGO CITY SCHOOLS. 1982, *Bilingual demonstration project*. April.

SELIGER, H., KRASHEN, S. & LADEFOGED, P. 1975, Maturational constraints on the acquisition of second language accent. *Language Sciences*, 36, 20–22.

SHAPSON, S. M. & DAY, E. 1982, A longitudinal evaluation of an early immersion program in British Columbia. *Journal of Multilingual and Multicultural Development*, 3, 1–6.

STERN, H. H. 1963, *Foreign languages in primary education*. UNESCO.

STERN, H. H., SWAIN, M. & MCLEAN, L. D. 1976, *Three approaches to learning French*. Toronto: OISE Press.

STEVENS, F. 1976, *Second language learning in an activity-centered program*. M.A. thesis, Department of Educational Technology, Concordia University.

SWAIN, M. 1978, French immersion: Early, late or partial? *The Canadian Modern Language Review*, 34, 577–85.

— 1981, Linguistic environment as a factor in the acquisition of target language skills. In R. ANDERSON (ed.), *Second language acquisition and use under different circumstances*. Rowley, Mass.: Newbury House, 109–22.

TRITES, R. 1981, *Primary French immersion: Disabilities and prediction of success*. Toronto: OISE Press.

TUCKER, G. R., HAMAYAN, E. & GENESEE, F. 1976, Affective, cognitive and social factors in second language acquisition. *The Canadian Modern Language Review*, 23, 214–66.

TUCKER, G. R., LAMBERT, W. E. & D'ANGLEJAN, A. 1972, *Are French immersion programs suitable for working class children? A pilot investigation*. Department of Psychology, McGill University.

4 Bilingualism and cognitive functioning

Jim Cummins
The Ontario Institute for Studies in Education

Abstract. The many seemingly contradictory findings regarding the effects of bilingualism on cognitive and academic functioning are reviewed. It is suggested that the "threshold" hypothesis may help resolve these apparent contradictions. This hypothesis proposes that the levels of proficiency that bilingual children attain in their two languages may be important intervening variables in mediating the effects of bilingualism on cognitive and academic functioning. Specifically, bilingualism may have positive effects on cognitive and academic development if a certain minimum or threshold level of bilingual proficiency is attained but negative effects if the individual develops low levels of proficiency in both languages. The original version of this hypothesis is refined by making a distinction between long-term and short-term effects of bilingual experiences and also by relating the cognitive effects of bilingualism more closely to the social context.

A large majority of studies conducted between 1920 and 1960 reported that, in comparison to unilingual children, bilingual children tended to perform more poorly at school, score lower on the verbal parts of intelligence (IQ) tests and exhibit more emotional problems (see Darcy, 1953; Peal & Lambert, 1967). Investigators often spoke of "mental confusion" and "language handicaps" among bilingual children and some writers went so far as to claim that bilingualism led to split personalities and schizophrenia (see Diebold, 1968) and that bilinguals were morally untrustworthy (see Vildomec, 1963).

Many of these early studies were poorly designed in that they failed to take into account the effects of confounding variables, such as socio-economic status (SES). For example, in some studies middle-class unilingual children were compared with lower-class bilingual children. However, the trend in the research findings was so one-sided that it is not surprising that the risks associated with bilingualism and bilingual education should be uppermost in the minds of educators. This is illustrated in the brief from the Association of (English-speaking) Catholic Principals of Montreal (1969) which stated:

> "We are of the opinion that the average child cannot cope with two languages of instruction and to try to do so leads to in-security, language interference, and academic retardation." (Quoted in Lambert & Tucker, 1972)

Although the early studies often lacked adequate controls, the findings appeared very plausible because the scholastic difficulties of some groups of bilingual children were, and are, very obvious to educators. For example, the Coleman Report (Coleman, Campbell & Hobson, 1966) found that Spanish-speaking and native Indian children in the United States were considerably behind national U.S. norms in academic skills. Another current example is Finnish migrant children in Sweden who were reported to be characterized by "semilingualism", that is, their proficiency in both Finnish and Swedish (as measured by standardized tests) was very much below Finnish and Swedish norms (Toukomaa & Skutnabb-Kangas, 1977).

The phenomenon that many children who have grown up in a bilingual environment experience academic difficulties and identity conflicts requires explanation whether we attribute it to bilingualism or to some other factor. However, these negative findings must be interpreted in the light of the large number of research studies which have reported a positive association between bilingualism and cognitive and academic functioning (see Cummins, 1978a, for a detailed review). For example, children in French immersion programs (see Genesee, Chapter 3) have been found to perform better than comparison groups in some aspects of English skills (Barik & Swain, 1976; Swain, 1975; Tremaine, 1975). A positive association also has been found between bilingualism and both cognitive flexibility (Balkan, 1970) and divergent or "creative" thinking abilities (Cummins & Gulutsan, 1974; Scott, 1973) and some studies have reported that bilingual children are more advanced in general intellectual development than are unilingual children (Bain, 1975; Liedke & Nelson, 1968; Peal & Lambert, 1967). There is also evidence that bilingual children are better able to analyze linguistic meaning and are more sensitive to aspects of interpersonal communication than unilingual children (Bain, 1975; Ben-Zeev, 1977a, 1977b; Cummins, 1978b; Cummins & Mulcahy, 1978; Feldman & Shen, 1971; Genesee, Tucker & Lambert, 1975; Ianco-Worrall, 1972).

In a recent book entitled *The Bilingual Brain*, Albert & Obler (1979) conclude on the basis of the neuropsychological research findings that:

> "Bilinguals mature earlier than monolinguals both in terms of cerebral lateralization for language and in acquiring skills for linguistic abstraction. Bilinguals have better developed auditory language skills than monolinguals, but there is no clear evidence that they differ from monolinguals in written skills." (1979: 248)

These findings are not surprising when one considers that bilingual children have been exposed to considerably more "training" in analyzing and interpreting language than unilingual children. The greater analytic orientation to language of bilingual children is consistent with the view of Vygotsky (1962) who argued that the ability to express the same thought in different languages will enable the child to:

> "see his language as one particular system among many, to view its phenomena under more general categories, and this leads to awareness of his linguistic operations." (1962: 110)

Lambert & Tucker (1972) argued that a similar process was likely to operate among children in immersion programs. They suggested that as children develop high level bilingual skills they are likely to practice a form of "incipient contrastive linguistics" by comparing the syntax and vocabulary of their two languages.

How do we reconcile the findings that bilingualism is associated with both positive and negative cognitive and academic effects? Although few of the studies, either positive or negative, are without some methodological limitations, it does not seem possible to totally dismiss either set of findings on these grounds. Thus, we are left with the conclusion that bilingualism is a mediating variable which can be associated with either positive or negative consequences. An examination of the research studies suggests that Lambert's (1975) distinction between "additive" and "subtractive" bilingualism is relevant in this regard.

Additive and subtractive bilingualism

Lambert (1975) pointed out that a large majority of early studies were carried out with immigrant or minority language children whose first language (L1) was gradually being replaced by a more dominant and prestigious second language (L2). He terms the resulting form of bilingualism "subtractive" in that bilingual children's proficiency in their two languages at any point in time is likely to reflect some stage in the subtraction of L1 and

its replacement by L2. Where schooling is totally through minority children's
L2 (e.g. English in Canada and the United States) frequently, after several
years, children themselves will appear to actively promote the replacement
process by using L2 as often as possible and sometimes even refusing to
speak L1 at home. In the past, this negative attitude on the part of minority
children toward L1 was encouraged by teachers and school personnel who
often regarded minority children's L1 as the cause of their academic difficulties and an impediment to the learning of L2. Minority children were
often punished for speaking their L1 in the school. For our purposes, the
important point is that many of the bilingual children involved in the early
"negative" studies are likely to have developed low levels of proficiency in
both their languages.

Lambert contrasts the "subtractive" bilingualism of many minority
language children with the "additive" bilingualism generally achieved by
children whose L1 is dominant and prestigious and in no danger of replacement by L2. This is the situation of Anglophone children in French immersion programs (see Genesee, Chapter 3; Halpern, Chapter 2). The bilingualism of these children is termed "additive" since another socially relevant
language is being added to the bilingual's repertoire of skills at no cost to
proficiency in L1. The majority of studies reporting cognitive advantages
associated with bilingualism have been carried out in contexts where
children have attained an additive form of bilingualism, that is, relatively
high levels of proficiency in both languages.

This analysis suggests that the level of proficiency bilingual children
achieve in their two languages may be an important factor in determining the
cognitive effects of bilingualism. This idea is elaborated in the "threshold"
hypothesis (Cummins, 1976).

The threshold hypothesis

The threshold hypothesis proposes that there may be "threshold" levels
of linguistic proficiency which bilingual children must attain both in order to
avoid cognitive disadvantages and to allow the potentially beneficial aspects
of becoming bilingual to influence cognitive growth. This hypothesis
assumes that those aspects of bilingualism which might positively influence
cognitive growth are unlikely to exert a significant long-term effect until the
child has attained a certain minimum or threshold level of proficiency in
both languages. Conversely, if bilingual children attain only a very low level
of proficiency in L2 or L1, their range of potential interaction with the
environment through that language is likely to be limited (see Figure 1).

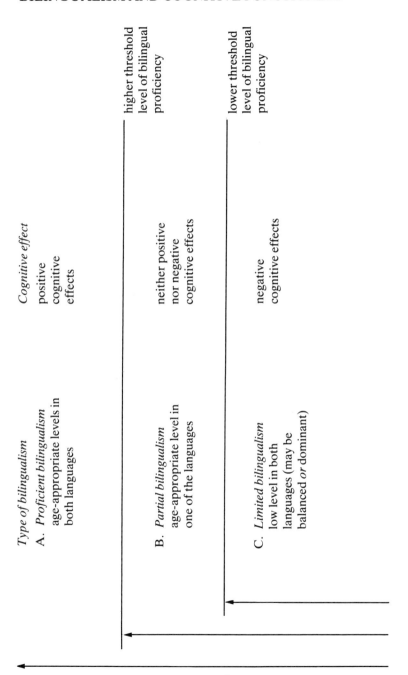

FIGURE 1 *Cognitive Effects of Different types of Bilingualism.*
(Adapted from Toukomaa & Skutnabb-Kangas, 1977)

The form of the threshold hypothesis most consistent with the available data is that there is not one, but two thresholds (Cummins, 1976; Toukomaa & Skutnabb-Kangas, 1977). The attainment of a lower threshold level of bilingual proficiency would be sufficient to avoid any negative cognitive effects but the attainment of a second, higher, level of bilingual proficiency may be necessary to lead to long-term cognitive benefits. Essentially, the hypothesis of a lower threshold level of bilingual proficiency proposes that bilingual children's proficiency in a language can be sufficiently weak so as to impair the quality of their interaction with their educational environment through that language. Thus, the early findings of negative cognitive effects associated with bilingualism would be explained by the fact that the minority language children in these studies often failed to develop a sufficiently high level of proficiency in the school language to benefit fully from their educational experience.

The more rapid cognitive and academic progress of bilinguals reported in recent studies would be explained by these children attaining the upper threshold level of bilingual proficiency, that is, high levels of both L1 and L2 skills. The threshold hypothesis would predict that neither positive nor negative cognitive effects would result from "dominant bilingualism" where children develop age-appropriate proficiency in their dominant language but achieve only intermediate levels of proficiency in their weaker language.

Refinements to the threshold hypothesis

Short-term and long-term effects

The threshold hypothesis is relevant only to long-term effects of bilingualism, that is, effects which result from actually functioning bilingually over a prolonged period of time. In other words, proficiency in L1 and/or L2 becomes important for cognitive development only when it is necessary to use L1 and/or L2 to interact with the environment over a prolonged period. Thus, in the initial stages of immersion programs (see Genesee, Chapter 3) children's proficiency in L2 is extremely low but they quickly attain a sufficiently high level to benefit fully from L2 instruction and to function bilingually in both academic and interpersonal contexts. In contrast, for reasons to be considered later, some minority children never seem to develop sufficient L2 proficiency to benefit fully from L2-only instruction (see Cummins, Chapter 5). This condition is cumulative and the children fall progressively further behind in academic and cognitive skills because their low level of L2 proficiency limits the scope of their interaction with the conceptual environment in school.

However, it is possible to distinguish between long-term effects of bilingual functioning and short-term effects which may result from the second language learning experience itself. The defining characteristic of a short-term effect of the process of acquiring proficiency in L2 is that it does not effect a fundamental or permanent change in an individual's cognitive functioning. Whether or not short-term effects will exert a more permanent long-term influence may depend on the type of bilingual proficiency attained. The distinction between short-term and long-term effects can be illustrated by recent research studies.

One example of short-term effects comes from an evaluation of a project in Munich in which French was taught for about half an hour per day to German kindergarten children. The lessons were taught by native French speakers and the children were encouraged to learn French by means of stories, actions, games and pictures as in Canadian immersion kindergarten programs. After the eight month test period the children could use about fifty French words in simple grammatical form. However, the L2 learning experience also seems to have affected children's use of their mother tongue. The report summarizes the effects as follows:

> "The 225 children who had taken the French course were better able to concentrate on the essentials when retelling stories, they did not beat about the bush and their formulations were preciser and more succinct than those of the 161 children who had not taken the foreign language." (Nordwest Zeitung, 28 April, 1979)

These effects on L1 story retelling seem likely to be a direct result of constructing meaning on the basis of a few cues (the words which were understood plus gestures and pictures) in listening to French stories. The essentials, but not the details, of the French stories would be assimilated. However, these effects are very unlikely to represent a fundamental change in cognitive functioning. If the French program were discontinued after kindergarten, it is unlikely that any group differences would be evident at the end of grade one.

Another example comes from a study conducted in the context of the Ukrainian–English bilingual program (50% Ukrainian, K to grade six) in Edmonton, Alberta (Cummins & Mulcahy, 1978). Three groups of children were compared on a variety of language processing tasks. One group of children in the program had extensive Ukrainian at home and were judged by their teachers to be relatively fluent in Ukrainian (*Bilingual Group*). A second group had little Ukrainian at home and were judged by teachers to have relatively little fluency in Ukrainian (*L2 Learners*). The third group was a unilingual English group attending regular classes in the same schools as the bilingual program students. All three groups were matched on non-verbal IQ and SES and were also equivalent in English reading skills. Among the measures administered were: the Semantic-Phonetic Preference Test, which was developed by Purbhoo & Shapson (1975) on the basis of a similar task used by Ianco-Worrall (1972); a word association test; and the Ambiguities Test which was taken from Kessel (1970) and assessed children's sensitivity to lexical, surface structure and underlying structure ambiguities.

The results for the Semantic–Phonetic Preference Test indicated that the grade one *L2 Learners* were less semantically and more phonetically oriented than the other groups. This finding is probably due to the necessity to "train one's ear" and attend to phonetic similarities and dissimilarities in the initial stages of the bilingual program. The fact that this is a short-term relatively superficial effect is confirmed by the fact that there were no differences among the three groups at the grade three level.[1]

On the other two measures, significant differences were found between the *Bilingual Group* and the other two groups of students. It is suggested that these differences represent more long-term effects since the bilingual children had been functioning bilingually for a considerable period of time. The finding that the bilinguals at both grade levels took longer to respond on the word association task agrees with Ben Zeev's (1977b) finding and suggests that bilinguals may process the semantic information more deeply than the other groups. It is also possible that generation of a response is more difficult for the bilinguals as a result of linguistic interference.

The other interesting finding was the superiority of the *Bilingual Group* in analyzing the dual meanings of ambiguous sentences. Here again the differences were evident at both grade one and grade three and represent more than just a superficial short-term effect. The finding that bilinguals are characterized by a more analytic orientation to language is consistent with many other studies (see Cummins, 1978a; Swain & Cummins, 1979).

Further examples of the differences between short-term and long-term effects can be taken from immersion programs. In late immersion programs, temporary lags in subject matter taught through L2 are sometimes found. However, by the end of the second year of the program those lags have usually disappeared and thus represent a short-term phenomenon which can be attributed to the process of acquiring proficiency in L2. However, a somewhat different phenomenon is the finding that at the end of elementary school, children in a partial immersion program (50% French, grades one to six) were performing more poorly than comparison groups in science and mathematics. Swain (1978) suggests that this may be because their level of French was not adequate to deal with the more sophisticated level of mathematical and scientific concepts being presented to them in French (see Genesee, Chapter 3). This would represent a long-term effect since the development of children's proficiency in French may not have kept pace with the conceptual demands of the curriculum.[2]

In conclusion, it is possible to distinguish between long-term effects of actually functioning bilingually over a considerable period of time and short-term effects of the L2 learning experience itself, i.e. the process of developing proficiency. The threshold hypothesis is relevant only to the former.

Varieties of bilingual proficiency

The threshold hypothesis does not specify what constitutes "high" and "low" levels of bilingual proficiency. Indeed, it is probably not possible to do this in any absolute sense since the threshold levels are likely to vary as a function of the conceptual demands of the situation and the intensity of exposure to the weaker language (see Cummins, 1976). However, it is possible to distinguish different levels of proficiency within a language; for example, immigrant children may maintain speaking fluency and listening comprehension skills in L1 but develop L1 literacy skills only to a minimal degree if these are not explicitly taught. Thus, it may be possible to relate the effects of bilingualism to the types of L1 and L2 proficiency developed by the individual. This proficiency will be a function of the use made of different aspects of L1 and L2.

Some support for this hypothesis comes from a study carried out by Aitken (1978). Aitken tested 64 Canadian born unilingual English speakers and 50 Canadian born bilingual students whose L1 was not English on the listening comprehension and structure subtests of the Comprehensive English Language Test (CELT). All students were attending regular English classes in grades eight to eleven in the same schools. It was found that on the listening subtest the bilingual group performed significantly better than the unilingual group but the order was reversed on the structure subtest. The listening subtest primarily involves comprehension of taped discourse while the structure subtest taps reading and syntax knowledge assessed by a multiple choice cloze procedure. A possible interpretation of the differences between listening and structure subtests is that they reflect the bilingual students' probable weaknesses in their L1. These students are likely to have maintained interpersonal communicative skills in L1 but most will have developed literacy skills in L1 only to a minimal degree.

In conclusion, any positive or negative cross-lingual influences are likely to reflect the levels of proficiency developed by the bilingual in different aspects of L1 and L2. Thus, enhancement of overall literacy skills as a result of bilingualism will be possible only in situations where literacy skills have been developed in both languages. However, as Aitken's results suggest, the development of fluent interpersonal skills in two languages may also have some cognitive/linguistic effects.

Social context and development of bilingual proficiency

The distinction between additive and subtractive bilingualism is useful in delineating a gross difference between bilingual acquisition contexts and has clear implications for the development of bilingual proficiency. However, the distinction fails to explain the very large differences in educational performance between groups of minority language children in subtractive situations. Not all groups of minority language children perform poorly at school; in fact, studies carried out by the Toronto Board of Education (Ramsey & Wright, 1970; Rogers & Wright, 1969; Wright, 1971) show that, with the exception of children whose mother tongue is French, minority language children who were born in Canada tended to have higher academic achievement and were more likely to be in high academic streams than unilingual children, born in Canada, whose mother tongue was English. It seems likely that high parental aspirations play a major role in explaining the strong academic performance of these minority language children born in Canada.

However, for groups of minority children such as the French in Ontario (see King & Angi, 1968, and Wright, 1971), the Finns in Sweden, and Hispanic and Indian children in North America, substantial deficits in educational achievement have been reported. These findings cannot be wholly accounted for by the notion of subtractive bilingualism since the minority language children in the Toronto Board of Education studies are also in subtractive situations. An examination of global trends in the educational achievement of minority language children suggests that the groups who perform poorly in school are those who have been discriminated against economically and educationally and, as a consequence, are characterized by insecurity in relation to their own language and culture and ambivalence towards the dominant language and culture of the society (Cummins, Chapter 5). The effects of these sociohistorical factors on cognitive/academic achievement are mediated through the types of proficiency children develop in L1 and L2.

Conclusions

It has been suggested that the long-term effects of bilingualism on academic and cognitive progress are a function of the type of bilingual proficiency developed by the individual. This, in turn, is largely determined by the social and educational context. However, there may be short-term effects of becoming bilingual on cognitive functioning which are relatively independent of both levels of bilingual proficiency and of the social and educational context.

Notes to Chapter Four

1. Ianco-Worrall (1972) found that 4–6 year-old bilingual students were more semantically oriented than an equivalent group of unilingual students; however, there were no group differences at the 7–9 age level. Since both grade one and grade three groups in the present study are closer to the age range of Ianco-Worrall's older group, the present findings do not contradict hers.
2. This finding appears to be specific to the particular partial immersion program evaluated by Swain (1978) and is not generalizable to all partial immersion programs (see Cummins, in press).

References

AITKEN, K. G. 1978, Comprehensive English Language Test. *TESL Talk*, 10, 1–4.

ALBERT, M. L. & OBLER, L. L. 1979, *The bilingual brain*. New York: Academic Press.

ASSOCIATION OF CATHOLIC PRINCIPALS OF MONTREAL, 1969, A Brief to the Commission of Inquiry on the position of the French language and on language rights in Quebec. Montreal. June.

BAIN, B. C. 1975, Toward an integration of Piaget and Vygotsky: Bilingual considerations. *Linguistics*, 160, 5–20.

BALKAN, L. 1970, *Les effets du bilinguisme francais-anglais sur les aptitudes intellectuelles*. Bruxelles: Aimav.

BARIK, H. C. & SWAIN, M. 1976, *Bilingual Education Project: Evaluation of the 1975–76 French Immersion Programs in Grades 3 to 5 (Ottawa and Carleton Board of Education)*. Toronto: Ontario Institute for Studies in Education.

BEN-ZEEV, S. 1977a, The influence of bilingualism on cognitive development and cognitive strategy. *Child Development*, 48, 1009–1018.

— 1977b, The effects of Spanish–English bilingualism in children from less privileged neighborhoods on cognitive development and cognitive strategy. *Working Papers on Bilingualism*, 14, 81–122.

COLEMAN, J. S., CAMPBELL, E. & HOBSON, C. 1966, *Equality of educational opportunity*, Washington, D.C.: U.S. Government Printing Office.

CUMMINS, J. 1976, The influence of bilingualism on cognitive growth: A synthesis of research findings and explanatory hypotheses. *Working Papers on Bilingualism*, 9, 1–43.

— 1978a, The cognitive development of children in immersion programs. *The Canadian Modern Language Review*, 34, 855–83.

— 1978b, Bilingualism and the development of metalinguistic awareness. *Journal of Cross-Cultural Psychology*, 9, 131–40.

— 1981, *Bilingualism and minority language children*. Toronto: OISE Press.

— 1983, Biliteracy, language and French immersion. *Canadian Journal of Education*, 8, 117–38.

CUMMINS, J. & GULUTSAN, M. 1974, Some effects of bilingualism on cognitive functioning. In S. CAREY (ed.), *Bilingualism, biculturalism and education*. Edmonton: The University of Alberta Press.

CUMMINS, J. & MULCAHY, R. 1978, Orientation to language in Ukrainian–English bilingual children. *Child Development*, 49, 1239–1242.

DARCY, N. T. 1953, A review of the literature on the effects of bilingualism upon the measurement of intelligence. *Journal of Genetic Psychology*, 82, 21–57.

DIEBOLD, A. R. 1968, The consequences of early bilingualism in cognitive development and personality formation. In E. NORBECK, D. PRICE-WILLIAMS & W. M. MCCORD (eds), *The study of personality*. New York: Holt, Rinehart & Winston.

FELDMAN, C. & SHEN, M. 1971, Some language-related cognitive advantages of bilingual five-year olds. *Journal of Genetic Psychology*, 118, 235–44.

GENESEE, F., TUCKER, G. R. & LAMBERT, W. E. 1975, Communication skills of bilingual children. *Child Development*, 46, 1010–1014.

IANCO-WORRALL, A. 1972, Bilingualism and cognitive development. *Child Development*, 43, 1390–1400.

KESSEL, F. 1970, The role of syntax in children's comprehension from ages six to twelve. *Monographs of the Society for Research in Child Development*, 35.

KING, A. J. C. & ANGI, C. E. 1968, Language and secondary school success. Ottawa: Royal Commission on Bilingualism and Biculturalism, Queen's Printer.

LAMBERT, W. E. 1975, Culture and language as factors in learning and education. In A. WOLFGANG (ed.), *Education of immigrant students*. Toronto: Ontario Institute for Studies in Education.

LAMBERT, W. E. & TUCKER, G. R. 1972, *Bilingual education of children: The St. Lambert experiment*. Rowley, Mass.: Newbury House.

LIEDKE, W. W. & NELSON, L. D. 1968, Concept formation and bilingualism. *Alberta Journal of Educational Research*, 14, 225–32.

NORDWEST ZEITUNG, 1979, Oldenburg, Germany, 28 April.

PEAL, E. & LAMBERT, W. E. 1967, The relation of bilingualism to intelligence. In J. MICHEL (ed.), *Foreign language teaching: An anthology*. New York: Macmillan, 143–91.

PURBHOO, M. & SHAPSON, S. 1975, *Transition from Italian*. Toronto: Toronto Board of Education, Research Report No. 133.

RAMSEY, C. & WRIGHT, E. N. 1970, *Language backgrounds and achievement in Toronto schools*. Toronto: Toronto Board of Education, Research Report No. 85.

ROGERS, R. S. & WRIGHT, E. N. 1969, *The school achievement of kindergarten pupils for whom English is a second language: A longitudinal study using data from the study of achievement*. Toronto: Toronto Board of Education, Research Report No. 80.

SCOTT, S. 1973, *The relation of divergent thinking to bilingualism: Cause or effect?* Unpublished research report, McGill University.

SWAIN, M. 1975, Writing skills of grade 3 French immersion pupils. *Working Papers on Bilingualism*, 7, 1–38.

— 1978, French immersion: Early, late or partial? *The Canadian Modern Language Review*, 34, 577–85.

SWAIN, M. & CUMMINS, J. 1979, Bilingualism, cognitive functioning and education. *Language Teaching and Linguistics Abstracts*, 12, 4–18.

TOUKOMAA, P. & SKUTNABB-KANGAS, T. 1977, *The intensive teaching of the mother tongue to migrant children of pre-school age and children in the lower level of comprehensive school.* Helsinki: The Finnish National Commission for UNESCO.

TREMAINE, R. V. 1975, *Syntax and Piagetian operational thought.* Washington, D.C.: Georgetown University Press.

VILDOMEC, V. 1963, *Multilingualism.* Sythoff-Leyden.

VYGOTSKY, L. S. 1962, *Thought and Language.* Cambridge, Mass.: M.I.T. Press.

WRIGHT, E. N. 1971, *Programme placement related to selected countries of birth and selected languages.* Toronto: Toronto Board of Education, Research Report No. 99.

The Schools' Response to Multiculturalism

5 The minority language child

Jim Cummins
The Ontario Institute for Studies in Education

Abstract. The purpose of this chapter is to describe first, the responses of school systems in the western industrialized countries to minority language children; second, the psycho-educational assumptions underlying these responses; and third, the research evidence relating to the validity of these assumptions. It is concluded that the findings of recent research studies and evaluations run counter to many of the implicit assumptions of educators concerned with minority language children. Specifically, these findings suggest that intensive teaching of the majority language is not necessarily the most appropriate form of educational treatment for groups of minority language children who tend to perform poorly in school.

During the past ten years a massive process of reorientation has begun in the school systems of the major Canadian cities. Two developments have combined to bring about this process: the federal policy of multiculturalism; and the extremely rapid increase in the numbers of immigrant students in urban school systems. The aims of the multiculturalism policy for education are to find effective ways of realizing the educational potential of culturally and linguistically diverse children and to develop social cohesion by promoting appreciation among all children of the varied contributions of different ethnic groups to the Canadian mosaic. The practical relevance of this policy has increased in recent years as the number of students who do not have English as a first language has grown to approximately 50% in the Toronto and Vancouver school systems. This phenomenon is common to most of the western industrialized countries. Chaib & Widgren (1976) estimate that by the year 2000 about one-third of the European population under 35 will have immigrant background.

71

The primary initial concerns of the reorientation process in Canadian schools have been to improve the teaching of English as a second language (ESL) and to develop curricula which would promote cross-cultural under-standing (Ashworth, 1975; Chapters 6–9 this volume). Since command of the English language is a prerequisite to the adjustment of immigrant children to the school environment and to Canadian society as a whole, the strong emphasis on improving the effectiveness of ESL instruction is clearly appropriate. However, there is a growing realization that ESL instruction cannot be treated as an isolated process but must be co-ordinated with an understanding of immigrant children's overall linguistic, psychological and educational development. Thus, in Canada as well as in the other western industrialized countries which have large numbers of immigrant children, educators have begun to broaden their focus in order to provide school programs which would address the needs and strengths of the total child rather than just deficiencies in the language of the host country.

Although virtually all educators would adhere to the principle of ad-dressing the needs of the total child, consensus breaks down when attempts are made to translate this principle into educational practice. Depending upon the relative significance attributed to different factors in explaining the poor educational performance of many monority group children (e.g. Bhatnagar, 1976; Coleman, Campbell & Hobson, 1966; Skutnabb-Kangas & Toukomaa, 1979; Verma & Mallicks 1978) the adaptations which educa-tors decide are required in the educational treatment could range from relatively minor changes, such as greater sensitivity to the child's cultural background and learning style, to major changes, such as the use of the child's home language as the primary medium of communication throughout elementary school.

Obviously, the political, social and administrative feasibility of differ-ent adaptations varies widely and these considerations must be balanced with an assessment of the educational needs of immigrant children. How-ever, because there is so little consensus as to what are the educational needs of immigrant children, and because very little research has been carried out, political, social and administrative factors have tended to play an overriding role in determining the extent of change which has been instituted in school systems in Canada and other western industrialized countries.

Minority languages in the school

The most contentious issue in policy debates in virtually all the western industrialized countries has been whether, and to what extent, the home language (L1) of minority group children should be incorporated into the school curriculum (e.g. Centre for Information on Language Teaching and Research, 1976; Epstein, 1977; Masemann, 1978; Smolicz & Secombe, 1977). The complexity of the issue can be seen in the fact that although psycho-educational, social policy, and administrative considerations must be weighed against one another, little consensus exists as to the probable effects of different options. For example, the primary rationale underlying bilingual education programs in the United States and Sweden is that the educational failure of many minority group children is a consequence of the mismatch between the language and culture of the home and of the school. The use of L1 as an initial medium of instruction is designed to ensure that academic progress is not retarded while the L2 is being learned. However, the validity of this rationale has been questioned on the grounds that the success of immersion programs for majority language children in Canada and elsewhere, shows that language mismatch, in itself, is not the crucial factor (Bowen, 1977; Epstein, 1977; Genesee, Chapter 3).

The social policy debate has centred on the issue of whether a policy of cultural pluralism which gave strong support for the maintenance of minority languages and cultures would lead to social fragmentation or, alternatively, encourage social cohesion (see debate in TESOL Newsletter, September, 1977). Related to this issue is the question of whether or not societal institutions are prepared to relinquish assimilationist goals.

The administrative and financial difficulties of providing instruction through the medium of L1 for children from a large variety of language backgrounds in the same schools have often been advanced as an argument against any change in the linguistic status quo. However, there are many examples throughout the world where administrative and financial considerations have not proven an insurmountable barrier to the recognition of children's L1 in the schools. For example, in Sweden it is obligatory for municipalities to organize mother tongue instruction if the children or their parents want it. By 1977/78, 41% of immigrant students were taught their mother tongues in the schools while 16% received auxiliary instruction in other subjects through the medium of their mother tongue (Skutnabb-Kangas & Toukomaa, 1979). In the United States bilingual education for minority language children is now wide-spread (Paulston, 1977; Tucker, Chapter 10 this volume), and a variety of bilingual programs for immigrant children also exist in Australia (Rado, 1978), the EEC countries (Appel, 1979; Willke, 1975) and in many developing countries (Tucker, Chapter 10).

How have Canadian policy makers responded to the "minority language" issue? The two major large-scale initiatives that have taken place in Canada during the past few years are the Heritage Language (HL) program in Ontario and the Programme d'Enseignement Langues d'Origines (PELO) in Quebec. The HL program involves teaching community languages either outside regular school hours or in the course of an extended school day for up to 2½ hours per week. More than 85,000 children (figures supplied by Ontario Ministry of Education) were participating in this program in 1982/83. The PELO project (Bosquet, 1979) involves teaching Italian, Portuguese, Greek and Spanish to children of these backgrounds for 30 minutes per day during regular school hours. In contrast to the HL program, the PELO is relatively small-scale involving about 1,600 children (1983/84).

The HL and PELO programs have incorporated minority languages into the school system as subjects of instruction. However, there also exist several programs in which minority languages are used as media of instruction. Among these are the Hebrew, English and French trilingual programs (Genesee, Tucker & Lambert, 1978) and the Ukrainian–English, and German–English bilingual education programs started in Edmonton in the early 1970s (Lamont, Penner, Blowers, Mosychuk & Jones, 1978) and currently spreading rapidly in Manitoba. Unlike the majority of children in the HL and PELO programs, most of the children in these trilingual and bilingual programs are third-generation immigrants whose home language is English. For example, in the Edmonton Ukrainian–English program only about 15% of children are fluent in Ukrainian on entry to the program. The aims of these programs are to give children an appreciation of the minority culture and to permit them to become functionally bilingual. Thus, the programs have similar aims to those of French immersion programs (see Genesee, Chapter 3) and can be categorized as "enrichment" programs in Fishman's (1976) terms.

Finally, there exist programs in which the minority language is used as an instructional medium in the initial stages of schooling as a "bridge" or transition to instruction through the L2. An example of this type of program in the Canadian context is the transition program operated by the Toronto Board of Education for Italian-speaking children (Shapson & Purbhoo, 1977).

Clearly, each of these types of program embodies certain psycho-educationalassumptions regarding the needs and potential strengths of minority language children. To what extent are different sets of psycho-educational assumptions supported by empirical evidence? What weight should be attached to different psycho-educational considerations in balancing them against possibly conflicting administrative, social or political considerations? If research were able to demonstrate convincingly that a particular form of educational adaptation (e.g. bilingual education) greatly increased the chances of educational success for certain types of minority language children, then the moral imperative to institute that form of education could become more difficult to evade on other grounds.

Two types of psycho-educational rationales have been advanced to justify the inclusion of minority children's L1 in the school curriculum. These rationales can be termed "L1 as transition" and "L1 as enrichment" respectively (see Fishman, 1976). The "transition" rationale, which underlies U.S. and Swedish bilingual education policy, is that the use of L1 as an initial medium of instruction is necessary to bridge the cultural and linguistic gap between home and school. The "enrichment" rationale points to the beneficial personal, emotional, and possibly cognitive effects of becoming highly competent in two languages and of being able to participate fully in two cultures. This type of rationale underlies immersion programs for majority language children (see Genesee, Chapter 3) as well as maintenance programs for minority children (e.g. Francophone minorities outside of Quebec).

Program options for minority language children

Table 1 presents the main types of educational programs for minority language children which are either in existence or have been proposed in terms of their assumptions (explicit or implicit) regarding the significance of L1 instruction for transitional or enrichment purposes. The purpose of making these assumptions explicit is to provide a basis for comparing different program options in terms of empirical research evidence and also to evaluate the extent to which different programs are likely to meet their psycho-educational goals.

The first alternative refers to the regular L2 program where no concessions are made either to the minority child's language or cultural background. This approach, which until recently was almost universal, has been termed "submersion" both to highlight its "sink or swim" philosophy and to distinguish it from the approach used in immersion programs for majority language children (Cohen & Swain, 1976). The approach is totally assimilationist and children's home language and culture are viewed either as impediments to educational progress or as having no functional significance.

The second alternative, the culturally sensitive program, is perhaps the most common approach to minority language education in the western industrialized countries. Efforts are made to broaden the cultural base of the school system and to generate respect for cultural diversity (see Chapters 6–9). Educational difficulties which minority children encounter are viewed

TABLE 1 *Assumptions Regarding Significance of Home Language and Culture in Programs for Minority Language Children*

Programs	Transition		Enrichment	
	Cultural	Language	Cultural	Language
1. "Regular" (submersion) (L2 only, no cultural adaptations)	−	−	−	−
2. Culturally Sensitive Regular (L2 only, + cultural adaptations)	+	−	+	−
3. Culturally Sensitive Regular +L1 Instruction (L1 taught as subject, e.g. HLP)	+	(−)	+	+
4. Culturally Sensitive L2 Immersion+L1 Maintenance (L1 used as medium for about 30% of time after L2 established)	+	−	+	+
5. Transitional Bilingual (L1 phased out as L2 established)	+	+	−	−
6. Language Shelter (L1 used as a major medium through schooling)	+	+	+	+

+ = factor viewed as significant
− = factor viewed as not significant
( )= with qualifications

mainly as a function of their deficiency in the language of the host country combined with the cultural mismatch between home and school.

Provision of minority language instruction at the elementary level as in the HL and PELO programs, has both cultural and linguistic goals. Culturally, it is intended to transmit a message to children that their language and heritage are worthwhile and valid and need not be rejected in favour of the dominant language and culture. It is expected that the cultural gap between the home and school will be narrowed and children will be encouraged to develop a healthy identification with both cultures. From a linguistic perspective, minority language instruction is intended to encourage the child to maintain L1 skills and to become literate in that language. However, in general, the HL and PELO programs do not embody transitional linguistic goals since subject matter instruction is through the medium of L2.[1]

The "Multilingual Project" (Rado, 1978) in Australia can also be classified under the third program option, although up to now it has been implemented only at the secondary level.[2] The project has developed parallel multimedia modules in both English and community languages on a variety of topics (e.g. Australian aborigines, computers) and children have the option of following the material in either language. Evaluation of the project has been very positive and the approach appears to have wide potential applicability.

The fourth alternative is that suggested by Cohen & Swain (1976) and by Epstein (1977) and would involve introducing the L1 as a medium of instruction for part of the school day after basic proficiency has been attained in L2 through an "immersion" approach. This approach derives from the successful French immersion programs in Canada (Lambert & Tucker, 1972; Genesee, Chapter 3; Swain, 1979) and would involve, among other things, initial segregation of minority and majority group children, and teachers who understand children's L1. Thus, in the early stages of L2 acquisition, children would be enabled to use L1 for communication among themselves and with the teacher, although the teacher would speak only L2 to the children. In comparison to a regular "submersion" program this "immersion" approach is likely to lessen the cultural mismatch between home and school; however, the academic aspects of linguistic mismatch are not considered significant. In other words, it is not considered necessary to teach subject matter in L1 while L2 is being acquired. As far as "enrichment" goals are concerned, the use of L1 as a medium of instruction in this program is likely to be more successful in promoting functional bilingualism than the teaching of L1 as a subject in, for example, the HL and PELO programs (see Swain, 1974).

Transitional bilingual programs attach considerable significance to the initial cultural and linguistic mismatch between home and school and use the child's L1 in the initial stages to allow curriculum content to be assimilated while L2 is being learned. Maintenance of L1 is not a program goal since L1 is no longer used as an instructional medium when the child's L2 skills are judged to be adequate to assimilate curriculum content through that language.

Programs in which the minority language is used as the major medium of instruction and the majority language is taught as a second language have been termed "language shelter" programs in Scandinavian countries (Toukomaa & Skutnabb-Kangas, 1977). Although, in terms of L1 and L2 usage in the early grades, language shelter programs may be indistinguishable from transitional programs, the goals and assumptions of the programs are very different. Proponents of language shelter programs (Hébert, 1976; Toukomaa & Skutnabb-Kangas, 1977) argue that effective promotion of conceptual development in both L1 and L2 and reinforcement of children's identity can best be achieved by using L1 as the major medium of instruction throughout elementary and secondary school. Thus, for language shelter programs, transitional and enrichment assumptions are not clearly distinguishable. The most obvious Canadian example is vernacular education for minority Francophone children. Language shelter programs share the same enrichment goals as French immersion programs for Anglophone children and "third" language programs such as the Ukrainian–English and German–English programs in western Canada. These goals are to produce children who are functionally bilingual (i.e. fluent and literate in two languages) and who can participate effectively in two cultural groups.

Empirical and theoretical considerations

A first principle in examining the appropriateness of different program options is that minority language children do not constitute a homogeneous group, either in terms of input to school systems or in terms of output. There are large differences both within and between groups of minority language children on entry to school, in terms of background factors, L1 and L2 abilities, motivation to learn L2 and maintain L1, as well as in other cognitive and attitudinal variables. Thus, different forms of educational treatment will exert a differential impact on children with different input characteristics. In other words, there is an interaction between educational treatment and child input variables. It is only by making this assumption that it is possible to account for the fact that under any form of educational treatment some minority language children appear to succeed relatively well whereas others fail.

If we ignore the fact that the six program options outlined in Table 1 differ in the extent to which they attempt to exploit the enrichment potential of the child's home language and culture, and compare them only in terms of the major goal which they share, that is, the development of high levels of L2 skills, then it follows from the interaction assumption that the six program options will be differentially effective in realizing this goal for students with different input chartacteristics. In other words, for some children who may, for example, be highly motivated to learn L2 and to identify with members of the dominant culture, a culturally sensitive L2 immersion program may be more effective, in terms of L2 learning, than a language shelter program that provides less intensive exposure to L2. However, for a minority child who is experiencing conflict and ambivalence vis-à-vis home and school cultures, a language shelter program may provide a better basis for L2 learning.

What evidence is there to support the transitional and enrichment rationales and what impact are the different program options likely to have on minority children's educational development?

Cultural identity and educational treatment

There is little controversy regarding the disruptive effects that cultural conflicts can have on minority children's academic adjustment (see Ashworth, 1975; Bhatnagar, 1976; Ramcharan, 1975) and most school systems in the western industrialized countries have made efforts (sometimes only token) to narrow the cultural gap between home and school. Lambert (1967) has distinguished four possible ways in which minority language children can work out their identity in relation to participation in two cultures:

(a) harmonious identification with both L1 and L2 cultures;
(b) identification with L2 culture, rejection of L1 culture (evidenced in, for example, unwillingness to speak L1);
(c) identification with L1 culture, rejection of L2 culture:
(d) failure to identify strongly with either culture.

These patterns of identification are intimately tied up with the learning of L1 and L2. For example, a child who identifies closely with both cultures is more likely to achieve high levels of proficiency in both languages than a child who identifies with neither.

In terms of enrichment goals only the first pattern of cultural identification is likely to promote comfortable participation in both cultures and high levels of L1 and L2 skills. Children who conform to the second pattern may perform well in school and gain high levels of L2 skills but at a cost to their L1 proficiency and possibly to familial harmony. Thus, if cultural enrichment is perceived as a desirable and feasible goal for minority children it is necessary to investigate the extent to which different program options lead to the first pattern of identification. If L1 cultural maintenance is not viewed as an important goal or is perceived as incompatible with L2 cultural identification, then the second pattern of identification would be considered acceptable or desirable. Informal observation suggests that this pattern is a common one among immigrant children in Canada and elsewhere. The extent to which initiatives such as the HL and PELO programs will promote a shift from the second to the first pattern identified by Lambert is an important issue in evaluating these programs.

The third and fourth patterns identified by Lambert (1967) seem to be associated with academic failure among minority children. An examination of the academic performance of different minority language groups in several countries shows a strong tendency for those groups who perform poorly in school to have ambivalent or negative feelings towards the L2 culture and often also towards their own culture. This pattern has been clearly documented for Finnish immigrants in Sweden by Skutnabb-Kangas & Toukomaa (1976). For, example, they quote Heyman's (1973) conclusion:

> "Many Finns in Sweden feel an aversion, and sometimes even hostility, towards the Swedish language and refuse to learn it under protest. There is repeated evidence of this, as there is, on the other hand, of Finnish people — children and adults — who are ashamed of their Finnish language and do not allow it to live and develop." (1976: 29)

Given this ambivalence, it is not altogether surprising that Finnish children born in Sweden perform extremely poorly in school; nor is it surprising that Finnish immigrant children who arrive in Sweden at age 10 or later who have not experienced this ambivalence and negative stereotyping in their pre-school and early schooling years perform better in Swedish language skills within a relatively short time as compared to those born in Sweden (Skutnabb-Kangas & Toukomaa, 1976).

It seems probable that the same ambivalence toward L1 and L2 cultures is a factor underlying the poor school achievement of many North American native groups. For example, Rosier & Farella (1976) report that, prior to the implementation of a bilingual program, Navajo Indian children in Rock Point and other Navajo schools were between 1.4 and 2 years behind U.S. norms in English reading by the end of grade six, despite intensive teaching of ESL.

The same factor might explain the otherwise puzzling Canadian findings of program stream placements of English, and French, and other minority language children in the Toronto Board of Education (TBE) who were born in Canada (Wright, 1971). First, minority language groups born in Canada showed a greater proportion of students in high academic program streams than groups whose mother tongue was English. This tendency existed across all socio-economic categories for groups such as Italian, Chinese, Ukrainian and German. Second, the French group showed a high proportion of students in low academic streams at both elementary and secondary levels. This tendency was again apparent across socio-economic levels but French-speaking students born outside Canada did not show this pattern (Wright, 1971).

The relatively high educational achievement of bilingual children born in Canada has been documented in other TBE reports (e.g. Ramsey & Wright, 1969) and it seems likely that high parental aspirations play a major role in explaining these findings. For these groups, any cultural conflicts that may have been experienced have clearly not proved debilitating as far as educational achievement is concerned. However, for the French group this is not the case and it seems likely that their relatively low achievement is related to the ambivalence felt towards their own language and culture vis-à-vis the dominant English language and culture. This ambivalence on the part of parents is likely to affect both their patterns of interaction with and their aspirations for their children. This in turn may exert a negative effect on children's linguistic and academic development.

"Caste" minorities and academic achievement

The notion of "bicultural ambivalence" is consistent with the structural analysis of minority student academic failure provided by Ogbu (1978). Although Ogbu's analysis is not directly concerned with language education, the patterns of minority children's performance he identifies shows clearly the futility of looking only at linguistic or school program variables for explanations of the effects of bilingual programs.

Ogbu first distinguishes among three types of minority groups: autonomous, caste and immigrant minorities. Autonomous groups possess a distinct racial, ethnic, religious, linguistic or cultural identity and are generally not subordinated economically or politically to the majority group. Jews and Mormons are examples of autonomous groups in the United States.

Caste minorities, on the other hand, are usually regarded by the dominant group as inherently inferior in most respects. Their post-educational opportunities are restricted to the least desirable social and occupational roles and their failure to ascend the socio-economic ladder is attributed to inherent characteristics of the group (e.g. "innate intelligence", "cultural deprivation", "bilingualism"). Ogbu identifies Black, Indian and Hispanic groups in the United States as caste minorities and attributes their school failure to inferior education combined with their perception of economic barriers ("job ceiling") which limit the rewards to be gained from formal education:

> "Caste minority children naturally acquire the linguistic, cognitive, motivational, and other skills or personal attributes adaptive to their adult roles. These skills may promote their failure in the dominant group's type of school success, but in that very way

schooling improves their adaptability to the menial social and occupational roles they will play as adults." (Ogbu, 1978: 41)

Immigrant minorities differ from most caste minorities in that they have moved into a host society more or less voluntarily and tend to have instrumental attitudes towards the host society and its institutions. They tend to be less affected by the ideology of dominant group superiority than are caste minorities and often their lot appears to be very good compared to that of their reference group in the homeland. Ogbu gives Chinese and Japanese as examples of such immigrant groups in the United States. He also points out that the status of minority groups may change. The fact that recent Finnish immigrants to Sweden and Mexican immigrant workers in the United States manifest the characteristics of caste minorities is clearly a function of historically determined patterns of relationships between the cultures. For example, Finnish immigrants to Australia are regarded as a high status group and perform well academically (Troike, 1978) thereby fitting the description of "immigrant" rather than "caste" groups, in contrast to their counterparts in Sweden.

Ogbu's distinctions between different types of minority groups and his structural analysis of the causes of school failure among caste minorities is clearly compatible with the "bicultural ambivalence" notion and helps explain the poor school performance of Franco-Ontarian students relative to other minority language students in Ontario. They also permit the Canadian findings to be related to findings in other educational contexts.

Several recent research projects suggest that language shelter programs have been effective in promoting educational success for minority students who tend to fail in L2-only programs. Before reviewing these research findings, it is necessary to consider the role of linguistic factors as intervening variables in bilingual children's academic and cognitive development.

Linguistic factors and educational treatment

Functional bilingualism as enrichment. There is no question that becoming fluent and literate in a language or languages other than one's mother tongue significantly increases an individual's potential for personal development. Much of the popularity of French immersion programs in Canada (see Genesee, Chapter 3) can be attributed to this factor. Throughout the world individuals spend vast amounts of time and money learning second languages. This activity is strongly promoted by educational and other institutions in order to increase the linguistic resources of the society. Given the obvious individual and societal benefits of bilingualism, one might ask why the already developed linguistic resources represented by community languages are not cultivated to a greater extent. The major reasons in most cases are clearly sociopolitical; however, these reasons have often been cloaked in the garb of psychological rationalizations concerning the negative effects of bilingualism and bilingual education. Assimilationist educational policies have been justified on the grounds that bilingualism leads to academic retardation and language handicaps.

Certainly there was empirical evidence to suggest that bilingualism was associated with lower levels of verbal intelligence (see Darcy, 1953; Peal & Lambert, 1967). However, there was until relatively recently, little inquiry as to why these negative effects were always found among immigrant and minority language children; whereas the bilingualism of majority language groups or "elitist" bilingualism (Fishman, 1976) had never been an educational problem. This phenomenon is exemplified in Canada by the success of French immersion programs. In Lambert's (1975) terms, educationally successful forms of bilingualism tend to be "additive" in that the individual adds an L2 at no cost to L1 proficiency. The bilingualism of minority language groups is termed "subtractive" in that the child's L1 skills are replaced or "subtracted" in the process of acquiring L2.

The findings of a considerable number of recent studies suggest that additive forms of bilingualism can positively influence academic and cognitive functioning (see Cummins, Chapter 4). While any cognitive advantages associated with additive bilingualism are likely to be fairly subtle and not represent large-scale enhancement of cognitive growth, the evidence supporting such effects does add an extra dimension to the obvious personal advantages of functional bilingual skills. The educational policy implications of this analysis are embodied in the issue of how to change the educational environment of minority language children such that additive rather than subtractive forms of bilingualism are developed. Program options 3, 4, and 6 in Table 1 are the only ones that aspire to this type of "enrichment" objective. However, is it realistic to talk of "enrichment" objectives given the fact that many groups of minority language children exhibit a high rate of school failure? The issues underlying this question are related to the transitional assumptions of the program options in Table 1.

L1 instruction as transition. A major issue underlying the transitional assumptions of the six program options in Table 1 is whether the educational failure of many minority language children can be wholly accounted for by cultural mismatch between home and school or whether linguistic factors also play a significant role for some children. It is possible to distinguish three basic positions on this issue. The position underlying options 1–4 is that minority children's conceptual and academic development can be adequately mediated by L2; consequently, it is not essential to use L1 as an instructional medium for the initial grades although some instruction through L1 may be desirable for cultural identity reasons or to maintain basic skills in L1 (options 3 and 4). The position underlying transitional programs (option 5), on the other hand, is that academic and conceptual development can be adquately mediated by L2 only after a certain level of L2 skills has been attained. The theoretical and practical problem with this position is, of course, to specify what is the minimum level of L2 skills required to benefit from L2 instruction and, on this basis, to establish entry and exit criteria for transitional programs. The language shelter approach (option 6) takes the position that minority children's L1 should be the major medium of instruction throughout schooling, but especially in the early grades, since this represents the most effective means of promoting both secure cultural identity and overall conceptual development, thereby providing a basis for the assimilation of both L2 and academic content. For advocates of language shelter programs, functional bilingualism is the only realistic educational goal for minority language children; the alternative for many children, it is argued, is "semilingualism", that is, low levels of language proficiency in both languages (Skutnabb-Kangas, 1978; Toukomaa & Skutnabb-Kangas, 1977).

At this stage it is not possible to draw any final conclusions on the validity of the theoretical assumptions underlying most of these program options. Whether options 3 and 4 would be successful in reducing the disproportionate numbers of children from some minority language groups who fail in school under options 1 and 2 is not known because examples of the third option are relatively recent and most have not yet been evaluated while option 4 has not been put into effect in any minority language situation. In general, transitional programs in the United States appear to have met with only limited success (Paulston, 1977). However, it is not possible to say to what extent this apparent limited success is a function of invalid theoretical assumptions, poorly implemented programs or poorly designed evaluations (e.g. American Institutes for Research, 1977; Leyba, 1978; Swain, 1979).

Language shelter programs. Several recent projects suggest that the "language shelter" approach is particularly effective for children who are experiencing ambivalence vis-à-vis home and majority cultures. As noted previously, intensive teaching of the majority language has not produced encouraging results in minority language groups such as the Finns in Sweden, native Indian children in North America, or minority Francophone children in some parts of Canada. This is illustrated in a quotation from a Swedish school psychologist:

"After a certain amount of L2 teaching, it doesn't matter how much more such teaching you give some of the immigrant kids. They do not progress. It is as if they reach a cognitive limit." (quoted by Ekstrand, 1978: 63)

There is a striking contrast between this arrested state of cognitive and linguistic development under L2-only instruction and the progress made by some groups of minority children when L1 is used as the major medium of instruction in the early grades. Consider some examples.

The preliminary results of a large-scale longitudinal evaluation in Sodertalje in Sweden suggest that by the end of grade six, Finnish immigrant children who have been initially instructed mainly through Finnish, with Swedish becoming a major medium of instruction only from grade three, perform almost as well as Swedish L1 children in Finland on Finnish and Swedish language tests (Hanson, 1979). The findings from other studies of bilingual programs for Finnish children are consistent with these results (Lasonen & Toukomaa, 1978; Toukomaa & Skutnabb-Kangas, 1977).

Bilingual programs for children of migrant workers have also been implemented in Holland with similar results. Appel (1979), for example, compared the Dutch language proficiency of two groups of Turkish and Moroccan migrant workers' children, one of which was receiving instruction mainly through L1 while the other received instruction either mainly or totally through Dutch. It was found that after 8 months in school, children who were instructed mainly through L1 were just as proficient in Dutch as those instructed through Dutch.

The findings of the longitudinal evaluation of the bilingual program for Navajo students at Rock Point in the United States are also consistent with the assumptions of language shelter progrms (Rosier & Farella, 1976). Since 1971, the school at Rock Point has operated a bilingual curriculum in which all initial literacy skills are taught in Navajo, and English reading is introduced only after Navajo reading skills are well established (in grade two). The evaluators of the bilingual program at Rock Point compared how students in the program were performing relative both to students at Rock Point School before the program was instituted and also to other Bureau of Indian Affairs (BIA) schools in the Navajo area which did not have bilingual instruction.

It was found that by grades five and six the Navajo students whose L1 skills had been promoted by the school were performing at the National U.S. norm in English reading. Before the bilingual program was instituted students at Rock Point were about 1½ years below the norm in English reading despite intensive ESL instruction in the school. Similarly, the BIA schools which did not have bilingual instruction were over 2 years below the national norm by the end of elementary school.

The grade two comparisons between Rock Point and the BIA schools are interesting. The Rock Point students who had been reading in English for only 5 months or less did just as well in English reading as BIA students who had at least 2 years of English reading experience. More important, however, is the fact that between grades two and six the Rock Point students' rate of growth in English reading skills was about double that of students in the BIA schools. Rosier & Farella attribute this increased rate of growth to bilingual instruction:

"It represents the cumulative effects of initial literacy in Navajo and the promotion of cognitive development through instruction in the native language. . . . The teaching of Science and of Navajo Social Studies in the Navajo language may have given students practice in critical thinking beyond the level accessible to them in a monolingual English curriculum." (1976: 387)

Findings from studies of minority Francophone students in Canada instructed through French show a similar trend. Carey & Cummins (1979) for example, reported that grade five children from French-speaking home backgrounds in the Edmonton Catholic School System bilingual program (80% French, 20% English, from K-12) performed at an equivalent level in *English* skills to Anglophone children of the same IQ in either the bilingual or regular English programs. An evaluation carried out by Popp (1976) showed that grade twelve minority Francophone students in Welland, Ontario who had been instructed mainly through French in the primary grades and for about 50% of the time in the secondary grades performed as well as Anglophone students (taught entirely through English) on measures of English reading comprehension but less well on measures of English vocabulary.

A large-scale study carried out by Hébert (1976) among grades three, six, and nine Francophone students in Manitoba also shows that there is no simple relationship between instruction through the medium of a language and achievement in that language. At all grade levels there was a significant positive relationship between percentage of instruction in French (PIF) and French achievement but *no relationship* between PIF and English achievement. In other words, Francophone students receiving 80% instruction in French and 20% instruction in English did just as well in English as students receiving 80% instruction in English and 20% in French.

The success of these programs suggests that the development of deeper levels of linguistic proficiency in both L1 and L2 is closely bound up with children's overall intellectual development and that conceptual skills developed in one language can easily be transferred to another (see Cummins, 1981). Thus, the psycho-educational assumptions of language shelter programs appear to have some validity. However, on the basis of studies to date it is not possible to disentangle the effects of the linguistic factor from those of the "cultural identity" factor. In other words, the success of these programs could derive either from helping minority children resolve their ambivalence in relation to home and school cultures or, alternatively, from the fact that:

> "development of the child's first language up to a capacity from abstraction provides the best conditions for acquiring a good knowledge of the second language and consequently, in the long run, for a successful schooling." (Willke, 1975: 367)

Clearly, these alternative explanations are not mutually exclusive. Also, in the case of language shelter programs, transitional and enrichment rationales cannot be neatly separated; in other words, well-developed L2 skills could be due either to the initial use of L1 as an instructional medium (transition) or to positive conceptual-linguistic consequences which, recent studies suggest, can result from attaining high levels of bilingual skills.

Conclusions

It is clear that there exists a variety of psycho-educational rationales for providing mother tongue instruction for minority children. These rationales often coexist with sociopolitical rationales such as facilitating the free flow of labour between countries and the return of the migrant worker to the home country at some point (Michalski, 1977). For the minority group itself cultural maintenance is usually the strongest motivating force. However, although the existence of a particular program is influenced by a large number of factors it is possible on the basis of the experience to date to draw tentative conclusions regarding some of the psycho-educational factors at work in determining the educational development of minority children.

First, there exists considerable variation between minority language groups in the extent to which children are capable of succeeding in an L2-only school milieu. This variation is independent of socio-economic status and appears to be related to sociocultural factors such as the degree of ambivalence vis-à-vis home and majority cultures. These sociocultural factors, in turn, result from sociopolitical and historical factors which have given rise to "caste-like" status for some minority groups.

Second, the "language shelter" approach appears to be effective in reducing school failure among minority children who tend not to succeed in an L2-only setting.

Third, the success of language shelter programs as well as of immersion programs for majority children suggests that in bilingual learning situations achievement in the majority language is minimally related to amount of instruction received through the medium of that language (see also, Genesee, Chapter 3). This appears to be because the majority language is reinforced in the wider community and instruction in the minority language is effective in promoting children's overall conceptual skills. However, instructional time in the minority language *is* significantly related to achievement in that language.

Fourth, the high level of academic achievement of minority children in some L2-only school settings (e.g. Bhatnagar, 1980; Ramsey & Wright, 1969; Wright 1971) shows that bilingual or language shelter programs are not "necessary" for all minority children. However, there is considerable evidence that the attainment of functional bilingual skills can positively influence children's cognitive functioning. These findings add an extra dimension to the obvious personal advantages of bilingualism and suggest that school systems should explore ways of exploiting this potential strength of minority language children. Highly successful functional programs of this type exist in western Canada.

Thus, recent research findings run counter to many of the intuitive assumptions of educators concerned with minority language children. Specifically, these findings suggest that intensive teaching of the majority language is not necessarily the most appropriate form of educational treatment for minority children who are performing poorly in school. Educational policy makers should therefore adopt a flexible, open-minded approach which takes account of the psycho-educational needs and potential strengths of minority children as well as of the cultural aspirations of their parents.

Acknowledgements

Preparation of this paper was made possible through financial support from the Multiculturalism Directorate of the Secretary of State, Ottawa. An earlier version appeared in *Interchange*, 1979/80, 10, 72–88.

I would like to thank Jean Handscombe, David Stern, and Merrill Swain for their valuable comments on an earlier draft of this paper.

Notes to Chapter Five

1. In some school systems the HL curriculum covers certain aspects of the regular curriculum and in this sense might be regarded as "transitional" since the same content is taught in L1 and L2.
2. The Multilingual Project clearly differs from the HL and PELO programs in that the language is not taught as a subject but used as a parallel medium to teach content. However, it has been grouped in this category because the time allocation and consequent overall impact are likely to be similar.

References

AMERICAN INSTITUTES FOR RESEARCH. 1977, Evaluation of the impact of ESEA Title VII Spanish/English bilingual education programs. Report submitted to U.S. Office of Education.

APPEL, R. 1979, The acquisition of Dutch by Turkish and Moroccan children in two different school models. Unpublished research report, Institute for Developmental Psychology, Utrecht.

ASHWORTH, M. 1975, *Immigrant children and Canadian schools*. Toronto: McClelland & Stewart.

BHATNAGAR, J. 1976, Education of immigrant children. *Canadian Ethnic Studies*, 8, 52–70.

— 1980, Linguistic behaviour and adjustment of immigrant children in French and English schools in Montreal. *International Review of Applied Psychology*, 1/2, 141–58.

BOSQUET, M. 1979, Le P.E.L.O. au Quebec: Les objectifs vises, les composantes de la phase experimentale et l'evaluation. Paper presented at C.S.S.E. Conference, Ragina, Saskatchewan.

BOWEN, J. D. 1977, Linguistic perspectives on bilingual education. In B. SPOLSKY & R. COOPER (eds), *Frontiers of bilingual education*. Rowley, Mass.: Newbury House.

CAREY, S. T. & CUMMINS, J. 1979, English and French achievement of grade 5 children from English, French and mixed French–English home backgrounds attending the Edmonton Separate School System English–French immersion program. Report submitted to the Edmonton Separate School System. April.

CENTRE FOR INFORMATION ON LANGUAGE TEACHING AND RESEARCH. 1976, *Bilingualism and British education: The dimensions of diversity*. CILT Reports and Papers, 14.

CHAIB, M. & WIDGREN, J. 1976, *Invandrarbarnen och skolan*. Stockholm: Washlstrom & Widstrand.

COHEN, A. D. & SWAIN, M. 1976, Bilingual education: The immersion model in the North American context. In J. E. ALATIS & K. TWADDELL (eds), *English as a second language in bilingual education*. Washington, D.C.: TESOL.

COLEMAN, J. S. CAMPBELL, E. & HOBSON, C. 1966, *Equality of educational opportunity*. Washington, D.C.: U.S. Government Printing Office.

CUMMINS, J. 1981, *Bilingualism and minority language children.* Toronto: O.I.S.E. Press.

DARCY, N. T. 1953, A review of the literature on the effects of bilingualism upon the measurement of intelligence. *Journal of Genetic Psychology*, 82, 21–57.

EKSTRAND, L. H. 1978, *Bilingual and bicultural adaptation.* Doctoral dissertation, University of Stockholm.

EPSTEIN, N. 1977, *Language, ethnicity and the schools.* Washington, D.C.: Institute for Educational Leadership.

FISHMAN, J. 1976, Bilingual education: What and why. In J. E. ALATIS & K. TWADDELL (eds), *English as a second language in bilingual education.* Washington, D.C.: TESOL..

GENESEE, F., TUCKER, G. R. & LAMBERT, W. E. 1978, An experiment in trilingual education. *The Canadian Modern Language Review*, 34, 621–43.

HANSON, G. 1979, The position of the second generation of Finnish immigrants in Sweden: The importance of education in the home language to the welfare of second generation immigrants. Paper presented at symposium on the position of the second generation of Yugo-slav immigrants in Sweden. Split. October.

HÉBERT, R. 1976, *Rendement academique et lange d'enseignement chez les eleves franco-manitobains.* Saint-Boniface, Manitoba: Centre de recherches du College Universitaire de Saint-Boniface.

HEYMAN, A. 1973, *Invandrarbarn: Slutrapport.* Stockholm: Stockholms Invandrarnamd.

LAMBERT, W. E. 1967, A social psychology of bilingualism. *Journal of Social Issues*, 23, 91–109.

— 1975, Culture and language as factors in learning and education. In A. WOLFGANG (ed.), *Education of immigrant students.* Toronto: Ontario Institute for Studies in Education.

LAMBERT, W. E. & TUCKER, G. R. 1972, *Bilingual education of children: The St. Lambert experiment.* Rowley, Mass.: Newbury House.

LAMONT, D., PENNER, W., BLOWERS, T., MOSYCHUK, H. & JONES, J. 1978, Evaluation of the second year of a bilingual (English–Ukrainian) program. *The Canadian Modern Language Review*, 34, 175–85.

LASONEN, K. & TOUKOMAA, P. 1978, Linguistic development and school achievement among Finnish immigrant children in mother-tongue medium classes in Sweden. University of Jyvaskyla, Department of Education. Research report No. 70.

LEYBA, C. F. 1978, Longitudinal Study Title VII Bilingual Program Santa Fe Public Schools, Santa Fe, New Mexico. Los Angeles: California State University, National Dissemination and Assessment Center.

MASEMANN, V. L. 1978, Multicultural programs in Toronto schools. *Interchange*, 9, 29–44.

MICHALSKI, C. 1977, Teacher education for a multicultural society: Some global trends and the Ontario Ministry of Education position. In V. D'OYLEY (ed.), *The impact of multi-ethnicity on Canadian education.* Toronto: The Urban Alliance on Race Relations.

OGBU, J. 1978, *Minority education and caste*. New York: Academic Press.

PAULSTON, C. B. 1977, Research viewpoint. In *Bilingual education: Current perspectives, Vol. 2. Linguistics.* Arlington Va.: Center for Applied Linguistics.

PEAL, E. & LAMBERT, W. E. 1967, The relation of bilingualism to intelligence. In J. MICHEL (ed.), *Foreign language teaching.* New York: Macmillan, 143–91.

POPP, L. A. 1976, The English competence of French-speaking students in a bilingual setting. *The Canadian Modern Language Review*, 32, 365–77.

RADO, M. 1978, What bilingual education can tell us. *Ethnic Studies*, 8, 42–50.

RAMCHARAN, S. 1975, Special problems of immigrant children in the Toronto school system. In A. WOLFGANG (ed.), *Education of immigrant students.* Toronto: Ontario Institute for Studies in Education.

RAMSEY, C. & WRIGHT, E. N. 1969, Students of non-Canadian origin: The relation of language and rural-urban background to academic achievement and ability. Toronto Board of Education. Research report No. 76.

ROSIER, P. & FARELLA, M. 1976, Bilingual education at Rock Point — some early results. *TESOL Quarterly*, 10, 379–88.

SHAPSON, S. & PURBHOO, M. 1977, A transition program for Italian children. *The Canadian Modern Language Review*, 33, 486–96.

SKUTNABB-KANGAS, T. 1978, Semilingualism and the education of migrant children as a means of reproducing the caste of assembly line workers. In N. DITTMAR, H. HABERLAND, T. SKUTNABB-KANGAS & U. TELEMAN (eds), *Papers from the first Scandinavian–German symposium on the language of immigrant workers and their children.* ROLIG-papir 12, Roskilde Universitetscenter.

SKUTNABB-KANGAS, T. & TOUKOMAA, P. 1976, Teaching migrant children's mother tongue and learning of the language of the host country in the context of the socio-cultural situation of the migrant family. Helsinki: The Finnish National Commission for UNESCO.

— 1979, Semilingualism and middle-class bias: A reply to Cora Brent-Palmer. *Working Papers on Bilingualism* 19, 181–96.

SMOLICZ, J. J. & SECOMBE, M. J. 1977, A study of attitudes to the introduction of ethnic languages and cultures in Australian schools. *The Australian Journal of Education*, 21, 1–24.

SWAIN, M. 1974, French immersion programs across Canada: Research findings. *The Canadian Modern Language Review*, 31, 117–129.

— 1979, Bilingual education: Research and its implications. In C. A. YORIO, K. PERKINS & J. SCHACHTER (eds), *On TESOL '79: The learner in focus.* Washington, D.C.: TESOL.

TESOL NEWSLETTER. 1977, Bilingual education: The continuing problem of communication, 11 (4), 21–22.

TOUKOMAA, P. & SKUTNABB-KANGAS, T. 1977, The intensive teaching of the mother tongue to migrant children of pre-school age and children in the lower level of comprehensive school. Helsinki: The Finnish National Commission for UNESCO.

TROIKE, R. C. 1978, Research evidence for the effectiveness of bilingual education.

Bilingual Education Paper Series, 2. Los Angeles: National Dissemination and Assessment Center.

VERMA, G. J. & MALLICK, K. 1978, Social, personal and academic adjustment of ethnic minority pupils in British schools. Paper presented at the International Congress of Applied Psychology.

WILLKE, I. 1975, Schooling of immigrant children in West Germany, Sweden, England. *International Review of Education*, 21, 357–82.

WRIGHT, E. N. 1971, Programme placement related to selected countries of birth and selected languages. Toronto Board of Education. Research report No. 99.

6 Implications of multiculturalism for curriculum

June Wyatt
Simon Fraser University

Abstract. Critical issues are raised about the goals of education in the multicultural society of Canada. The first section outlines classroom and community issues which arise from the fact that Canada is a multicultural society. Historical background and current points of view on these issues are presented. Recent developments in curriculum for multicultural education are then noted. The view presented is that the source of ethnic identity is the family and ethnic community; the school and the society at large must play a supporting role. Educators must provide minority students with opportunities to learn skills for survival in society without requiring abandonment of their cultural background.

Canada is a multicultural society and this fact raises critical questions about the goals of Canadian education. Should the aim of education be the assimilation, integration or segregation of minority groups? Is equality of educational opportunity achieved by educating all children in the same way regardless of differences in their cultural and linguistic backgrounds? Does this society desire equality of educational opportunity? These are questions facing educators in general. Related to these are specific questions of practical concern to teachers. Is a culturally, racially, and linguistically heterogeneous classroom viewed as a rich educational resource or a powder keg of discrimination and prejudice? What types of curriculum materials are appropriate for teaching in a multicultural society? Before an informed selection of possible approaches and materials can be made teachers must have a clear vision of the role they wish to take in the process of social and cultural change.

Classroom and community issues

The question of immediate concern to most teachers is "What can I do about racial and cultural discrimination in the classroom?" Immediate answers to this question can serve as strategies for inter-personal conflict resolution. Long range plans to deal with the issues take on a programmatic format; their design and methodology must be shaped in view of community issues such as the following:

— Why do children from minority groups generally reject their parents' language and cultural background — whether or not they are overtly discriminated against?

— Whose responsibility is it to maintain cultural traditions and languages: the school's or that of the parents and the community?

— Why are some minority group parents *NOT* in favour of cultural and linguistic maintenance?

The decisions which educators reach about these issues will be influenced in part by some social and educational certainties:

— It is clear that in many classes there are language barriers; children do not speak English as their first language (e.g. in the Toronto and Vancouver school districts approximately 50% of the school children come from homes where English is not the first language).

— Teachers are rarely prepared with the cross-cultural information necessary to know why many immigrant parents object to children taking a swimming class or going on overnight trips; why some Indo-Canadian boys wear their hair covered with a handkerchief; why some Chinese students will not look their teacher in the eye.

— Overt discrimination (e.g. name calling, physical assault, teasing, exclusion) does occur in some classrooms.

— Language differences and a shortage of community liaison workers account for the fact that there is little contact between the home and the school.

Most decisions about classroom and community issues will have to be made in the *absence* of certainty about some critical educational issues (e.g. the exact nature of the relationship between self-concept, ethnic identity, and academic achievement; the appropriate balance of control between school and community in reinforcing and supporting the continuity of culture and language).

Historical background and current points of view

The focus in this analysis is on two different but essentially liberal views of the role of education in a multicultural society: the assimilationist and the pluralist.

The former view is that the only way to insure social equality is by guaranteeing that all children receive the same educational programs. The latter advocates a highly diversified education system in which ethnic groups are provided with educational programming which draws on and helps develop their cultural background. Programs of this type become the foundation for knowledge and understanding of other cultures. In spite of their differences both these views contrast strongly with those which are explicitly discriminatory. Regardless of differences among themselves, liberal social scientists and educators are all battling a Canadian legacy of discrimination against minorities which persists into the present.

Discriminatory views

In 1946 Prime Minister of Canada, MacKenzie King, expressed the view that:

"The people of Canada do not wish to make a fundamental alteration in the character of their population. The government will therefore not permit large scale Asiatic or other 'colored' immigration."

Doug Collins (1979) formerly a columnist for the *Vancouver Sun* published *Immigration: The Destruction of English Canada* in which he echoed views expressed in a number of his earlier articles:

"Anyone naive enough to think that the massive cultural and racial mix we are heading toward is good, or at least harmless, should look at the European experience. There is a will and a need for this country to stay white because that is what people want. They can't tolerate other groups." (Collins, 1976: 10)

Highly visible among the intolerant and the subject of much recent media attention and public scrutiny is the Ku Klux Klan. It blatantly identifies itself as racist, targets various minorities as intellectually inferior and advocates a policy of subsidized repatriation of immigrant "undesirables". In a report on his investigations into their activities in British Columbia, McAlpine (1981) cautioned that the Klan was a threat which should be sanctioned by law (The Civil Rights Protection Act). He also cautioned that a more pervasive threat was the racism which, although not "rampant", does exist in the school system, law enforcement and government agencies, and in the public at large. McAlpine introduces his report by concurring with the findings of Patel (1980) which dismissed the contention that if we ignore racism it will go away:

> "The more fundamental problem (than the Klan *per se*) is the creation of an environment in which messages of racial supremacy and hatred on the grounds of race, religion and ethnic origin will not find a receptive audience." (McAlpine, 1981: 2)

Like many historians and social scientists before him (e.g. Allport & Kramer, 1946; Adorno, 1950; Milner, 1975), McAlpine is suggesting that the forces leading to discrimination in contemporary western society are complex and endemic, but we can, with legislation and education, keep them at bay.

Liberal views

Most significant of the contrasting liberal philosophies, because it is official federal policy on multiculturalism, is that presented in the Royal Commission Report on Bilingualism and Biculturalism (1970). As already mentioned by Shapson (Chapter 1), recommendations in this report made a broad statement for multiculturalism within a bilingual framework. Specific recommendations provided support for the teaching of languages other than English or French as options in the school program where there is sufficient demand.

Federal policy will be used as a reference point in analyzing the liberal views (assimilationist and pluralist) referred to earlier. How would the two opposing views be likely to evaluate this policy?

The assimilationist view has been put forward most strongly by the sociologist John Porter with Jean Burnet echoing some of his main points. Porter points out that ethnic origin can and has been used as a way of discriminating and that one of the positive elements of our educational system is that it places

> "emphasis on individualistic achievement in the context of a new nation with universalistic standards of judgement . . . it meant forgetting ancestry and attempting to establish a society of equality where ethnic origin did not matter." (Porter, 1975: 9)

On the other hand, Porter (1975) allows that the maintenance of language and group identification (but not culture) by minority groups has the positive function of providing a "psychic shelter", a protective resting place from which minority group members can begin the process of assimilating into Canadian society. Because the Report of the Commission on Bilingualism and Biculturalism stresses support for language activities (rather than cultural, social, political, or economic activities) Porter would probably favour it. He would not be especially supportive of the provision of such programming within the educational system. Language maintenance in his view should take place within the ethnic community; presumably to phase itself out once its "sheltering" function has been fulfilled.

Burnet (1979) has criticized the government policy:

"The name itself ('multiculturalism') implies something that is hardly possible: that many cultures can be maintained in Canada.

In fact, except for such isolated groups as the Hutterites, no ethnic group brings a total culture to Canada and none can maintain intact what it brings under the impact of the new environment. It is ethnic identity that can and does persist and selected cultural patterns as symbolic expressions of that identity . . . (On the other hand) cultural maintenance depends on *isolation*." (1979: 48)

Echoing this view, Vallee (1969) comments:

"The more a minority group turns in upon itself and concentrates on making its position strong the more it costs its members in terms of their chances to make their way as *individuals* in the larger system. Among ethnic minority groups which strive to maintain language and other distinctions, motivations to aspire to high ranking social and economic positions in the larger system will be weak." (1969: 95)

To these writers success in Canadian society is a function of individual achievement, and ethnic group ties are inhibitory. Thus the educational system must emphasize individualistic achievement rather than group solidarity.

Along these lines and directly relevant to education is the McGregor Commission Report: *The Education and Training of Teachers in British Columbia* (1978) which makes two brief references to multicultural education:

"The elementary teacher's professional training *must include* study of: (among other things) The history and philosophy of education. Here the student must be introduced to other cultures, especially those that have made major contributions to our own." (1978: 12)

"A number of alternative programmes for the training of teachers are administered by the Faculties of Education. These we are not proposing to eliminate, indeed most seem highly attractive. Nevertheless, it is Canadian culture that must stand firm as the bedrock of our educational system and our aim must be to assimilate new Canadians rather than to appease every claim for diversity. Not every demand justifies an alternative programme nor does every popular fad." (1978: 17)

Liberal pluralist educators will quickly point out that emphasis on assimilation and individualistic achievement is already the hallmark of our public schools and *still* minority group children are not rising in the social and professional structure of the country. They prescribe a different course of action based on a definition of culture which is quite different from that forming the basis of Burnet's view. They describe culture as dynamic — growing and changing — incorporating new elements and simultaneously abandoning some traditions; the new and the old exist side by side. Burnet's view on the other hand, implies that culture is *only* tradition; it is a style of life which takes the past as its reference point; its continuity consists of replicating this past. When she asserts that ethnic identity (rather than culture) persists it is not clear whether she thinks this ethnic identity is constructed purely from traditional forms or whether it allows the incorporation of new elements. The pluralist educational point of view stresses the dynamism of evolving ethnic identities, new adaptations and expressions of cultural forms in response to new environments. A basic premise is that many cultures can coexist (with the help of appropriate educational programs). In this regard they favour the recommendations of the Royal Commission because they allow for diversity. Disfavour is expressed because of tight budgetary restrictions and constraints on developments of language programs (other than English and French).

Quite in contrast to the assimilationists, pluralists point out that the foundation for individualistic achievement (so lauded by the assimilationists) is a positive feeling about one's ethnic identity. Consequently they argue that to ensure equality it is necessary for society and schools to support the formation of positive ethnic identity. Lind (1974) articulates a pluralist view. He feels that as a nation we pride ourselves on our pluralism but in fact our institutions and schools in particular are assimilationist.

"The rhetoric for Canadian culture is 'mosaic' but the reality of Toronto's education system is 'melting pot'. . . . An implicit

assumption of New Canadianism (the educational programs designed to teach English and Canadian culture to immigrants) is
that our social fabric is too fragile to withstand the onslaught of
multiple cultures.

. . . . The curriculum guideline series of the Ministry of Education set out the situation quite clearly. 'It's a question of seeing
the school as the institution for achieving social cohesion as over
against seeing it as the agency for personal fulfillment as the
ethnic groups desire'. That indeed is the question. (1974: 115)

The implications of the assimilationist view are that educational programming should be geared to fitting students into Canadian society quickly.
Towards this end it is necessary to minimize the reinforcement of differences. Programs which teach English as a second language (ESL) are
sufficient for achieving linguistic goals; any support for programming which
encourages diversity should come from and be conducted within the ethnic
community.

On the other hand it is the view of the pluralists that through appropriate programming both social cohesion of the society at large and ethnic
group desires can be fulfilled. This can be done in a variety of ways as
illustrated by multicultural education programs developed in recent years.
These can be divided into two groups: those which focus on minority
language instruction and those concerned with all other facets of the curriculum. Both the language and curriculum programs provide specific answers
to the initial questions raised in this paper about the appropriate role of
education and the educational system. Cummins has expressed a pluralist
view in dealing with language programs for minority children (Chapter 5).
The following section provides an introduction to other approaches to
multiculturalism in the school curriculum.

Multicultural curriculum: An introduction

Approaches to multicultural curriculum range from those which give
token recognition of holidays to integrated approaches where most subject
matter areas take multicultural mateiials and issues into account. Some
programs take a heritage/museum approach where the focus is on a group's
past and the primary objects of study are artifacts or material culture. Other
programs take an issues approach, or focus on themes like cultural change
taking a dynamic view of ethnicity and culture (see Connors, Chapter 7;
Werner, Connors, Aoki & Dahlie, 1977). Variation also exists in staffing
patterns; the range includes programs where there are no ethnic group
members involved in teaching or administration to those in which minority

group members have total control of administrative and teaching positions. Other variables affecting program design include: age of children and thus the appropriateness of various curriculum models, availability of staff, financing, sociopolitical climate, curriculum development skills, and educational and social philosophies of program developers.

A sampling of a variety of current curriculum for multicultural education reveals strong similarities in goals and objectives, all of which are liberal and pluralist in their philosophy.

The Scarborough (Ontario) Board of Education in the *Multiculturalism Teachers' Guide — Junior Division* (1977) states the goals of its program are:

"To make students aware of the different cultural groups that make up Canadian society;

To encourage children of ethnic groups to have pride in their heritage;

To foster understanding of and empathy with people of other cultural groups." (1977, Section 2, pp. 1–2).

This philosophy is echoed in *Multiculturalism in Action: Curriculum Ideas for Teachers*, published by the Ontario Ministry of Education (Breithaupt, Burke, Kane & Michalski 1977). The objectives of this program are to give each child an opportunity to:

"develop and retain a personal identity by becoming acquainted with the historical roots of the community and culture of his other origin, and by developing a sense of continuity with the past;

begin to understand and appreciate points of view of ethnic and cultural groups other than his or her own;

and at the same time to develop an understanding of such concepts as community, conflict, culture, and interdependence;

learn the social skills and attitudes upon which effective and responsible cooperation and participation depend." (1977: 2)

There are many other notable curriculum guides, texts and programs in Canada which articulate similar liberal-pluralist objectives (e.g. Bavington, Lithwick, Sproule & Thompson, 1979; Hood, 1980; N.W.T. Handbook for Curriculum Development, no date; Sheffe, 1975; Wood, 1978; Wood & Remnant, 1980). Current bibliographies and resource guides list hundreds of books for students which provide supplements and supports for these objectives (e.g. The Children's Book Centre, 1981; Canadian Book Information Centre, 1981).

The role of educators in a multicultural society

Amidst conflicting views, what is the proper role for the teacher? There are many with pluralist views who are hesitant to implement programs because they lack information about minority groups and skills for dealing with intercultural and racial conflict. They are fearful of community disapproval or of creating problems in classrooms where there is no apparent conflict. Some can see the value of multicultural education where the school or class is itself multicultural but question the utility of programming in a culturally homogeneous environment. What is an appropriate course of action?

Teachers must act, but they cannot always act alone. Many who wish to become involved need support, training and materials provided by school boards, universities and ministries of education. Others who do not see the need to become involved, or actively oppose involvement, at best might be swayed in their views as the system around them changes. At worst, we can only hope their impact will be minimized by the positive action of others.

A variety of curriculum models provide evidence that materials and strategies are available. The life experiences which provide the resources for these models must come from ethnic community members; a purely academic multicultural curriculum would quickly become arid. Implementing curriculum requires the joint efforts of educational personnel and ethnic group members.

Many critics of multicultural education assert that we are trying to preserve lifestyles which ethnic minorities themselves are discarding. The real issue is not preservation but development. Until very recently, ethnic minorities have not been provided with the opportunity for cultural development in (or outside of) Canadian educational institutions. We cannot say they have turned this option down because in fact it has never been offered. If educational institutions in Canada wish to maintain that they provide equal educational opportunity and teach the realities of Canadian history and contemporary society it is now their responsibility to offer this option and to take the initiative in working with minority groups and teachers to develop reflective and practical skills necessary to develop and implement programs.

The issues examined in this chapter provide the background necessary for individuals to reflect on and formulate their roles as educators. In the next chapter, Connors argues for a multicultural curriculum approach to be constructed within the framework of a critical reflective process.

References

ADORNO, T. W. 1950, *The authoritarian personality.* New York: Harper.

ALLPORT, G. & KRAMER, B. 1946, Some roots of prejudice. *Journal of Psychology,* 22, 9–39.

BAVINGTON, J., LITHWICK, B., SPROULE, W. & THOMPSON, N. 1979, *Cultures in Canada.* Toronto: MacLean Hunter.

BREITHAUPT, A., BURKE, M., KANE, B. & MICHALSKI, C. 1977, *Multiculturalism in action: Curriculum ideas for teachers.* Toronto: Ontario Ministry of Education.

BURNET, J. 1979, Myths and multiculturalism. *Canadian Journal of Education,* 4 (4), 43–58.

CANADIAN BOOK INFORMATION CENTRE. 1981, *Multiculturalism in Canada.* Vancouver: Canadian Book Information Centre.

THE CHILDREN'S BOOK CENTRE. 1981, *Canadian multicultural book for children.* Toronto: The Children's Book Centre.

COLLINS, D. 1976, Fear and loathing in the Canadian mosaic. *Vancouver Sun, Weekend Magazine,* September 11, 8–10.

— 1979, *Immigration: The destruction of English Canada.* Richmond Hill, Ontario: BMG Publishing.

Elementary education in the Northwest Territories: A handbook for curriculum development. Yellowknife: Government of the Northwest Territories, no date.

HOOD, B. 1980, *Teaching about likenesses and differences through film.* Vancouver: National Film Board of Canada.

LIND, L. 1974, New Canadianism: Melting the ethnics in Toronto schools. In G. MARTELL (ed.), *The politics of the Canadian public school.* Toronto: James Lorimer & Co.

MCALPINE, J. 1981, *Report arising out of the activities of the Ku Klux Klan in British Columbia.* Victoria: Government of British Columbia.

MCGREGOR COMMISSION REPORT. 1978, *The education and training of teachers in British Columbia.* Victoria: Government of British Columbia.

MILNER, D. 1975, *Children and race.* New York: Penguin Books.

Multiculturalism Teachers' Guide. 1977, Toronto: Scarborough Board of Education, Junior Division Program Department (History).

PATEL, D. 1980, *Dealing with inter-racial conflict: Policy alternatives.* Montreal: Institute for Research on Public Policy.

PORTER, J. 1975, Ethnic pluralism in Canadian perspective. In N. GLAZER & D. P. MOYNIHAN (eds), *Ethnicity: Theory and experience.* Cambridge: Harvard University Press.

ROYAL COMMISSION REPORT. 1970, *Bilingualism and Biculturalism Book 4: The Contributions of the other ethnic groups.* Ottawa: Queen's Printer.

SHEFFE, N. 1975, *Many cultures, many heritages.* Toronto: McGraw Hill-Ryerson.

VALLEE, F. 1969, The viability of French groupings outside Quebec. In M. WADE (ed.), *Regionalism in the Canadian community.* Toronto: University of Toronto Press, 83–89.

WERNER, W., CONNORS, B., AOKI, T. & DAHLIE, J. 1977, *Whose culture? Whose heritage?* Vancouver: University of British Columbia, Centre for the Study of Curriculum and Instruction.

WOOD, D. 1978, *Multicultural Canada.* Toronto: Ontario Institute for Studies in Education.

WOOD, D. & REMNANT, R. 1980, *The people we are.* Agincourt, Ontario: Gage Publishing.

7 A multicultural curriculum as action for social justice

Bryan Connors
University of Alberta

Abstract. Recurring difficulties most often encountered in the development of multicultural curricula are highlighted. A case is developed for an alternative curriculum approach to multicultural education based on social action.

Soon after publication of the Royal Commission Report on Bilingualism and Biculturalism (1970), the federal government officially recognized Canada as a multicultural society (House of Commons Debates, 1971). To many Canadians the word multiculturalism was ambiguous. Educational authorities and textbook publishers had no such doubt about multiculturalism. Troper (1976) noted that:

> "The very act of professing faith in the value of this ill-defined multiculturalism has virtually become an end in itself. Indeed, one suspects that almost any program can get approval, any expenditure authorized, if it is done in the name of multiculturalism." (1976: 3)

School curricula began to reflect the interest in multiculturalism; virtually all provinces across Canada introduced topics that contained elements of ethnic studies (see Wyatt, Chapter 6). Werner, Connors, Aoki & Dahlie (1980) observed that the inclusion of topics related to multiculturalism lacked any specific form or rationale; the content of multicultural programs was often arbitrary and had a tendency to focus on "exotic" groups often removed from the experience of the child. The National Council for Social Studies (1976) issued a position statement concerning guidelines for multi-ethnic education in an effort to restore or introduce some form of order to a particular curricula field. It was hoped that the guidelines would cause the

104

initiation of dialogue between the different educational parties who expressed an interest or concern with multicultural education programs.

Approaches to the multicultural curriculum

Aoki (1978) has suggested that educators examine the curricula approaches used by programs that stake a claim to being multicultural in character. Aoki (1978) observed that the dominant approach within multicultural education is one in which knowledge *about* ethnic groups is the primary focus of educators. Students are expected to acquire knowledge about the history and customs of selected ethnic groups. Werner *et al.* (1980) typify this approach to multicultural education by using the example of the "museum approach". The ethnic group under examination is objectified by educators who call upon students to "read about" and "study" an ethnic experience. Aoki (1977) has noted that such an approach is the transference of knowledge from expert sources (be it books, multimedia kits, or the teacher) to the head of the student. This orientation contains a view of the student as someone who needs to be filled with knowledge. The ethnic group under examination is viewed or looked at from the perspective of the outsider. The essence of this curriculum approach is "facts" about particular ethnic groups as gleaned from the work of experts.

A second curriculum approach is mentioned by Aoki (1978) in which ethnic studies programs can be constructed by using the framework of multiple interpretations. The focus is no longer on knowledge about an ethnic group and its experiences. The single voice of authority of an ethnic group's experience is no longer acceptable. The authoritative textbook is viewed as only one interpretation as this approach calls for multiple interpretations. The multiple interpretations curriculum approach demands that instructional materials be written from the insider's point of view, and recognizes that the perspective of an interpreter shades or colours the stance given toward an ethnic group or the concept of multiculturalism. In recent years this approach seems to have gained some recognition and is reflected in those textbooks or multimedia kits that juxtapose alternative interpretations. Aoki (1978) has noted that if Canada is to be committed to multiculturalism, then there has to be an acceptance within society that multiperspectives exist. It is only with the recognition that interpretation is allied to perspective that Canadians can seek to achieve any form of inter-ethnic communication. Students are called upon to analyze the interpretations presented within ethnic studies. Anyone who adopts the curriculum framework of multiple interpretations accepts the premise that heterogeneity is desirable. In seeking for an understanding and acceptance of diverse perspectives, one must believe that mutual respect is possible among diverse ethnic groups.

Aoki (1978) also addressed the question of a third curriculum approach where programs are constructed within the framework of a critical reflective process. The focus of the critical reflective process is dramatically different from the two approaches previously described. The prior curricula approaches are primarily concerned with knowledge about ethnic groups or with seeking an understanding of the perspectives by which ethnic groups' experiences have been interpreted. Aoki suggests that the intent of the critical reflective process is to create "more authentic human lives" (p. 97). Within the critical reflective curriculum framework, teachers and students are viewed as individuals who construct from their own world or social reality:

> "The focus is partly on the ethnic group studied, but to a greater extent it is on the subjective content of the teachers' and students' own consciousness. Within this focus the image each holds of the ethnic people studied is viewed as being also an image of himself." (1978: 97)

The critical reflective process calls upon the teacher and student to uncover their own perspective; the process in recognizing the constraining and distorting influence of perspectives makes it possible to "escape" perspectival bonds. The critical reflective framework allows the teacher and student to examine or discover the historical forces that have shaped an existing perspective. Aoki observes:

> "Thus by rendering transparent what has previously been hidden, criticism initiates a process of self-reflection designed to free oneself from the domination of past constraints. Criticism, thus, aims at changing the condition of what is false or distorted consciousness leading the self toward a more authentic mode of being." (1978: 98).

The critical reflective curriculum process allows the individual to transcend his personal ethnicity because an inter-subjective relationship can be developed with members of other ethnic groups. In reconstructing one's own world, it becomes possible to co-participate in the reconstruction of another's world.

Difficulties encountered in developing the multicultural curriculum

Aoki has described three curricula approaches to ethnic studies or multicultural education. Curriculum development, however, is also a political act. Werner (1977) states:

"This means that certain individuals and groups have the power to control the thinking of students and teachers by shaping conceptions of the society in which they live. In this way program developers become the gate-keepers of reality definitions. They select, classify, and evaluate viewpoints and knowledge for inclusion within programs. Certain perspectives are legitimized to the exclusion of other points of view." (1977: 48)

Program developers seem to have encountered some difficulty in determining what is meant by multiculturalism. Wangenheim (1976) sees the ambiguity of multiculturalism as a concept leading to incompatibility within specific curriculum approaches. This very ambiguity concerning the concept of multiculturalism may inadvertently have led to the development of programs that relied heavily upon traditional curriculum methodologies. In an effort to respond politically to multiculturalism, program developers have found it expedient to include multicultural content within existing programs or hastily prepared options. Aoki (1978) has provided the program developer with a view of three curriculum frameworks which vary significantly in their approach to multicultural education. Werner (1977) observes that the majority of multicultural programs across Canada rely upon one curriculum approach. Werner contends that the majority of multicultural programs were produced by experts and, as such, they are to be consumed by teachers and students. The curriculum developed by the "experts":

"Dispenses the proper information about multiculturalism and the legitimate images about ethnics for the student and for his community." (1977: 50–51)

The difficulty in accepting this approach is that the goal of the multicultural curriculum has been pre-determined. The teacher and student are called upon to absorb knowledge about multiculturalism. Action is viewed as something determined by others. Werner states:

"Images and conclusions concerning ethnicity are undirectionally shaped for and transmitted to the student and teacher, who in turn are expected to legitimate these values and interpretations." (1977: 50)

If we wish to seriously consider multicultural curriculum as action for social justice, an initial step requires a shift in the locus of power concerning curriculum decision making. To date little effort has been made towards the decentralization of curriculum development. It is true that isolated development, generally, remains firmly entrenched within departments of education. Wyatt (Chapter 6) has suggested that the life experience of ethnic group members be incorporated in the multiculturalism curriculum. Werner (1977) claims that only the Northwest Territories has accepted the devolution of power within multicultural curriculum development. The Northwest Territories' program has taken for granted local ethnic diversity and multicultural content attempts to build upon the various interpretative frameworks that exist within communities. The recognition of multiple perspectives and interpretations makes the Northwest Territories' program attractive. The program contains many of the features usually considered desirable where content features a multicultural reality. Whereas all too often multicultural studies are isolated from the rest of the school curriculum, this program was integrated within school programs. Integrated programs are often viewed as initiating dialogue between the ethnic groups that form a particular community. The respective ethnic groups residing within a community were considered co-producers of the resultant curriculum that became a part of the Northwest Territories' program. As Werner notes:

> "The result is a curriculum which has meaning in local situations and which is relevant to the various ethnic experiences. Meaning comes when ethnic realities are portrayed honestly, when there is opportunity for more than one interpretation of Canadian history and issues, and when local linguistic and cultural characteristics can be incorporated." (1977: 53–54)

The emphasis is on understanding and the action component of the program is the interaction between the different groups that make up a community. The groups have to work together in order to understand perspectives and the resultant interpretations, so that multicultural objectives can be achieved. The model adapted by such a multicultural program has within it the potential to achieve the third of Aoki's frameworks — that of the critical reflective process.

Social action and the multicultural curriculum

Aoki, when discussing the critical reflective framework as an approach to curriculum development, states:

> "We are hampered currently by our lack of competence in curriculum development within this kind of framework." (1978: 98).

The suggested approach as advocated by Aoki is a radical transformation from "accepted" curriculum development models. Paulo Friere (1970) considers virtually every educational endeavour a political act. The critical reflective framework calls upon the teacher and student to enter his own historical process as it relates to multiculturalism. The critical reflective framework requires that established meanings and values relating to multiculturalism be raised to a conscious level. There is a tendency for us to delete other views, distort messages we receive from others, oversimplify and generalize aspects of practical experience. The critical reflective framework calls upon teachers and students to venture communally by acting and critically reflecting upon experience. Wojtyla (1979) sees such an approach as emancipating the individual by exposing the taken-for-granted; such disclosure can lead to self-governance. Aoki (1980) notes that the classroom, within the critical reflective framework, should operate as a micro-community in which dialectical relationships exist. Communicative action within the micro-community is dependent upon recognizing intersubjectivity that is mediated through everyday language. Intersubjectivity seeks to illuminate the meaning given by teachers and students to multicultural programs. This endeavour to venture forth communally *is* action together. The critical reflection that such a framework calls for, while seeking to make an individual's historical processes conscious, also contains an action-seeking transformation not only at an individual level but also at a societal level. Gouldner (1974) sees the critical reflective framework as a binding together of reflection upon the world and the action to transform the world.

Friere (1970) claims that educators must examine how we have become what we are; the student must become an independent thinker. Providing programs that simply act upon and shape the consciousness of a student is to create an "a-historical" individual. Fay (1975) notes that educational practice is not deliberately one of dominance but rather something that is undertaken unwittingly. In rethinking the meaning of multicultural programs, the process of critical reflection becomes a catalytic agent. In examining multicultural programs and their meaning, questions can be raised that become the basis of teacher-student inquiry. What is meant by multiculturalism? Who determines the content and context of multicultural programs? Fay (1975) would ask questions of multicultural programs in terms of action. If multiculturalism is not an action from the student's own deliberations, then who demands it and for what purpose? Favaro (1981) claims that educational programs are often viewed in terms of problem solving. Favaro believes that in examining a concept such as multiculturalism our first concern should be "problematizing and should allow teachers to become co-participants in the process" (p. 26).

In an initial dialogue educators and students would examine present practice and would come to recognize the possibility of new approaches to the topic of multiculturalism. Dialogue would assist students in recognizing that individuals help construct a social-cultural reality. Words such as "multiculturalism", "action" and "social justice" could be used to initiate dialogue. The classroom becomes an action system; collaboration and group support would seem to be an essential, not only for dialogue to occur, but also to carry the tensions and anxieties that may arise as critical consciousness is developed. The group becomes a convivial centre as individuals engage their view of humanity. Fay sees such a group as being:

> "relatively small, relatively egalitarian (in the sense that no member has command over another without the other's approval), relatively free of recrimination between members, relatively committed to discussing its members' situations and experiences, and relatively insistent that its members take responsibility for whatever claims, decisions, or actions they undertake to make." (1977: 230)

In the classroom, students would examine multiculturalism, its current objectives and practice. Individual autobiographies could be constructed so that historical developmental processes could be relived; historical and sociological surveys could be undertaken, and enthnographies relating to issues affecting multiculturalism could become a feature of such programs. By such means it would be possible not only to describe multiculturalism but also to explain its relationship to contemporary society. The classroom as an action system engages the process of socialization and offers self-understanding and direction for change. Fay (1975) calls such an approach an educative model. The convivial group may articulate its satisfaction or dissatisfaction with multiculturalism. A vocabulary which conceptualizes existing situations in a multicultural society can be created. The ideology associated with multiculturalism can be examined within a definition of social justice, and commitment to action, hopefully, will become a reality.

Conclusions

Existing multicultural curricula are predominantly based on an approach in which students are required to gain knowledge and understanding of multicultural issues. This paper has proposed that, for commitment to multiculturalism to be centre-stage in the lives of students, an alternative curriculum approach based on social action is required. As an action system, the classroom of teacher and students would examine the historical process which creates each individual. The shared solidarity, when related to common experience, would plant the seeds of collective change. Based on the critical reflective framework (Aoki, 1980), this approach to multicultural curriculum would set out to develop in students a critical sense that would lead them to reflect on the multicultural society in which they live. The principal aim of such a curriculum is to awaken student consciousness to knowledge about the concrete situation within which they reside. The critical reflective approach is also of a practical nature; multiculturalism is "achieved" by action and participation on the part of the students.

References

AOKI, T. 1977, Theoretical dimensions of curriculum: Reflections from a micro-perspective. *Canadian Journal of Education*, 2, 49–56.

— 1978, Curriculum approaches to Canadian ethnic histories in the context of citizenship education. *The History and Social Science Teacher*, 13, 95–99.

— 1980, Toward a reconceptualization of curriculum implementation. Paper presented at the Summer Institute for Teacher Education. Burnaby, BC.: Simon Fraser University. July.

FAVARO, B. 1981, *Recasting a program in teacher education from a critical perspective*. Edmonton: University of Alberta.

FAY, B. 1975, *Social theory and practice*. London: George Allen.

— 1977, How people change themselves: The relationship between critical theory and its audience. In T. BALL (ed.), *Political theory and praxis: New perspectives*. Minneapolis: University of Minnesota Press.

FRIERE, P. 1970, *Pedagogy of the oppressed*. New York: Herder & Herder.

GOULDNER, A. W. 1974, Toward the new objectivity. *Theory and society: Renewal and critique in social theory* (Vol. 1). Amsterdam: Elsevier.

HOUSE OF COMMONS DEBATES. October 8, 1971, Ottawa: Government of Canada.

NATIONAL COUNCIL FOR SOCIAL STUDIES. 1976, *Curriculum guidelines for multi-cultural education: Position statement*. Arlington, Virginia.

ROYAL COMMISSION REPORT, 1970, *Bilingualism and Biculturalism Book 4: The Contributions to other ethnic groups*. Ottawa: Queen's Printer.

TROPER, H. 1976, Multiculturalism in the classroom: Pitfalls and Options. *The History and Social Science Teacher*, 12, 3–7.

WANGENHEIM, E. D. 1976, Multiculturalism and the curriculum: Official policy and local implementation. *The History and Social Science Teacher*, 12, 15–17.

WERNER, W. 1977, A study of perspectives on social studies. Doctoral Dissertation, University of Alberta.

WERNER, W., CONNORS, B., AOKI, T. & DAHLIE, J. 1980, *Whose culture? Whose heritage? Ethnicity within Canadian social studies curricula*. Vancouver: University of British Columbia, Centre for the Study of Curriculum and Instruction.

WOJTYLA, K. 1979, *The active person*. New York: Reidel & Dordrecht.

8 Multiculturalism and morality

Ian Wright and Carol LaBar
University of British Columbia

Abstract. A theoretical framework for multicultural education based on moral principles is developed. In order to understand the moral principles basic to multicuturalism, a distinction between cultural and ethical relativism is necessary, and certain knowledge, competencies, and dispositions are entailed. These include knowledge of the concepts of person, society, culture, prejudice and stereotyping; a sense of self-worth; and the ability to distinguish between factual and value claims, to identify points of view, to formulate valid arguments and to test moral principles. The claim is made that few programs in multicultural education have clearly delineated their moral stance, and thereby may rest on unsound assumptions. It is concluded that multicultural education must take into account the moral point of view in order that people can make rational decisions regarding life in a multicultural society.

Multiculturalism is a moral concern. Although it is defined in various terms — the education of recently arrived immigrants, support for cultural and community ventures, equal opportunity employment, the promotion of ethnic histories, the prevention of racism, and the encouragement of minority language instruction — multiculturalism has to do with how people of various cultural backgrounds are to be treated and how conflicts between people are to be resolved.

The announcement that multiculturalism within a bilingual framework would be federal government policy in Canada bears out this notion. Prime Minister Trudeau envisioned a society in which: members of all cultural groups would have equal economic, social, and political opportunities; the distinctiveness of a number of separate cultural groups would be encouraged and supported if these groups have "demonstrated a desire and effort to continue to develop a capacity to grow and contribute to Canada"; and national unity would be brought about by interaction among diverse cultural groups. (House of Commons Debates, 1971).

This vision of multiculturalism assumes that national unity can be brought about along with the maintenance of cultural diversity. This can create a tension between the laws, norms, and conventions needed to promote unity, and the beliefs and cultural practices of particular minority groups. Traditionally, in most countries, national unity has been brought about at the cost of, at least, some degree of assimilation to the country's dominant cultural norms. For any country to survive there must be agreement on certain basic procedural principles — there must be some common values and beliefs. Yet if attempts to develop common values are viewed as "cultural imperialism" or "assimilation", then multiculturalism is a forlorn hope.

How can this ideal society in which cultural diversity is encouraged and national unity promoted be brought about? How can a society in which persons are accorded certain rights, and are treated as "persons", in the moral sense of the term, be promoted? In order to help answer the above questions a distinction must be made between cultural relativism and ethical relativism.

Cultural relativism contends that different cultures embody different sets of values — different conceptions of "the good life". As Wright & Coombs (1981) state:

"Since there is no publicly acceptable evidence in terms of which any one conception of the good life can be shown to be truer than another, everyone is entitled to choose whatever conception she prefers *so long as she does not thereby treat others immorally or unjustly, or infringe upon another's right to choose her own conceptions of the good life.* Ethical relativism, on the other hand, claims not only that there are no grounds for choosing between conceptions of the good life, but further there are no grounds for preferring one set of *moral* ideals over any other. Thus, the ethical relativist would reject that part of the cultural relativist's claim *underlined* above because it contains a judgment based on a moral ideal." (1981: 3)

An example will help to demonstrate the distinction between cultural and ethical relativism, and will show that sometimes what may be commonly viewed as a cultural matter has moral implications. People dress in a variety of ways for a variety of reasons. Sometimes the reasons are based on economic, employment, or social factors; sometimes mere whim is the reason. Normally, the way people dress is of no moral significance. Thus we should not object in ordinary circumstances to a particular item of clothing. But a good case can be made that, for example, a long robe may lead to accidents in certain types of situations (e.g. in a place of work). In these situations a long robe may be objected to on grounds of safety. This cultural matter has become a moral matter because it has to do with the well-being of a person.

There are also cases in which one may object to a particular item of clothing (or another cultural symbol) because the clothing is related to particular beliefs. As stated earlier, normally the way people dress is not a moral issue. However, if one looks at the values embodied in the wearing of a veil by some Muslim women, then one may object, not to the veil *per se*, but rather to the beliefs it symbolizes (i.e. the subjection of women). Again, this seemingly cultural practice has moral significance because it affects, at least, the interests of Muslim women.

However, even though one may judge a particular cultural practice as immoral, the question remains as to whether it is justifiable to eliminate the practice when this might cause psychological harm to the practioners. In the above example, despite the relatively clear distinction between "cultural" and "ethical", the problem remains as to what is the morally right action.

Multiculturalism only makes sense if the cultural relativist view is adopted, and the ethical relativist view is rejected. If it is taken that people should be able to choose their own "good life", then this is only possible if ethical relativism is repudiated. One cannot choose a "good life" which infringes on the rights of others to choose their own "good life" without contravening the basic principle that all people should be able to choose. There have to be limits on choice, and these limits are based on moral principles which include such things as respect for persons, equal consideration for the interests of all people and not harming others unnecessarily.

We do not view these principles as merely norms of the majority culture. There are good reasons for members of all cultural groups to adopt them since they are basic to rational moral judgment. Teaching these moral principles would not count as forcing minority cultures to adopt the values of a majority culture. In fact, this teaching might require significnt changes in the values of the members of the majority culture or of minority cultures. Examination of the moral justifiability of cultural values might show that certain rules or norms are morally indefensible. Being born and raised in a particular culture does not necessarily entail that one *must* or *should* accept all the values of that culture.

The ideals inherent in multiculturalism oblige us to take a moral point of view, and to justify our policies and actions on the basis of moral principles. Morality requires that all people be treated equally unless there are relevant differences which justify unequal treatment (Hare, 1952; Peters, 1966). What constitutes a relevant difference is determined by various considerations. According to federal government policy, one such consideration is "a clear need for assistance" (House of Commons Debates, 1971). "Need" is a thorny problem. If a minority group needed food in order to avoid starvation we might well consider it the moral thing to do to provide food. However, what if members of a minority group claimed, on psychological grounds, that they needed to maintain a cultural identity, and asked for economic aid to fulfill this need? Then, according to government policy, this group must demonstrate "a desire and effort to continue to develop a capacity to grow and contribute to Canada" (House of Commons Debates, 1971). What criteria are to be used to determine the development of a capacity to grow and contribute to Canada? A capacity to grow might be viewed as an internal matter, that is, a minority group learns and understands more about its heritage, and individuals develop their potentials within the ethnic context. It could also be viewed externally, as for example through economic, religious, artistic, intellectual, political, or social contributions to Canada as a whole. Presumably it must be a positive contribution, but to whom? — to the majority of Canadians? to the least advantaged Canadians? to a particular group of Canadians?

It is these kinds of questions which require reasoned decision making. It is argued that in order to make reasoned decisions about life in a just multicultural society, one needs certain knowledge, dispositions and competencies.

Education and multiculturalism

Since 1971, efforts have been made to promote and implement multicultural programs in the nation's schools. These efforts have ranged from food festivals, ethnic histories, units of study on various minority groups, museum visits, the study of racism and prejudice, visits to classrooms by members of minority groups, and community service projects. It is our view that, in many cases, the objectives for such activities do not go far enough, or have not received enough serious reflection. For example, an ethnic food festival is presumably designed to show that people eat many different kinds of foods. However, behind this knowledge objective there appears to be the aim of demonstrating that this is "a good thing" in that different food preferences ought to be appreciated and respected. Whether or not students arrive at this appraisal is unknown. But more significant is the point that food choices may be based on economic factors and religious beliefs. There may be justifiable reasons for these choices which do not infringe on others' rights to make choices. Although there are exceptions (e.g. cannibalism) food preferences are usually a cultural matter. Yet, if students "succeed" in appreciating different culture's foods, are they then led to believe that they should appreciate all cultural differences? This, of course, brings us back to the importance of distinguishing between cultural and ethical relativism.

This approach to multicultural education, teaching the whats, hows and whys of human cultures, cannot be treated in a value neutral way. Whether only the material culture is studied, or the underlying beliefs and values of a culture are focused upon, teachers, through verbal or non-verbal means, will indicate how they judge the content (that some practices are desirable or undesirable; or that all practices are equally good). In addition, students also will make judgments. Unfortunately, they are rarely helped to make reasonable judgments. Exceptions are found in Wood & Remnant (1980) in which attention is paid to helping students use critical thinking skills in the study of multiculturalism, and in the proposed approach to multicultural curriculum as action for social justice (Connors, Chapter 7).

If it is taken for granted that multicultural education should consist of the study of various cultural groups living in Canada, then several approaches can be taken, each of which rests on differing assumptions. One can take an *outsider perspective* by comparing the culture under scrutiny with one's own, noting the similarities and differences. This approach emphasizes the material culture and the cultural distance between a majority and a minority group. By emphasizing differences it is easy to:

"objectify minority peoples, viewing them as peculiarities who stand apart from the mainstream of Canadian life." (Werner, 1981: 40)

Both similarities and differences are subject to evaluation, although it is probable that differences are subject to most appraisal. Theodore Newcomb, a social psychologist, has spent many years looking for ways to achieve peaceful coexistence between dissimilar groups. He points out that there is an association between "different" and "bad" and states:

"Ethnocentrism is born in the drive for (psychological) balance. The dilemma is how to maintain a culture's distinctiveness without promoting ethnocentrism and hostility. No one has solved it yet." (Quoted in Travis, 1974: 73)

In some research studies it has been found that students tend to reject those who are perceived as "backward" or "exotic" (Torney, 1977), and are more likely to acquire positive attitudes if similarities are accentuated (Williams & Salyachivin, 1973).

A person has to assimilate, accommodate and evaluate new information. One might take the view that any difference is all right for culture A, but not for one's own culture, or that it's right for everyone, or that it's right for no one. To judge this, one has to know what differences and similarities are relevant to determining how people ought to be treated. Some differences (and, for that matter, some similarities) may be morally justifiable; others may not. This point is vital to multicultural education. It has been assumed that, by studying ethnic history or by understanding the cultures of the various groups which constitute Canada, students will respect, appreciate and tolerate other people. But appreciation, tolerance, and respect can only be based on moral principles. If members of group A express their aesthetic needs in form B and this does not involve acting immorally toward anyone else, then it is justifiable to allow the continuance of B. But if group A believes that all non-As are inferior and should be discriminated against and harassed, then clearly this does infringe on the rights of others and as such is a moral concern.

Another approach to multicultural education is to take the *insider's perspective*. This perspective consists of attempting to put aside one's own cultural baggage and learn about the culture through the eyes of the partici-pants. This entails the ability to role-take in order to understand the experi-ence of others. The Van Nostrand Reinhold series (e.g. Ito, 1978; Burke, 1978; Mastrangelo, 1979) attempts to take the insider perspective by focus-ing on the experiences of immigrants through the eyes of the people in-volved. Yet even this series, at times, tends to become an examination of the problems immigrants encountered as they tried to fit into the majority cultural patterns.

Perhaps this insider approach can help us become aware of the roots of human beliefs and help us explore the concept of "humanness"; but perhaps also it can create a climate in which every culture because of its history, traditions, environment, and the perceived needs of its people are appraised as being "right". One might understand as fully as possible the caste system in India, but to view it as "right" because it was (and still is) a cultural factor is another matter. This argument taken to its logical conclusion, would lead us to accept the view that the Nazis were right and discrimination against certain minorities in Canada is right because they are, or were, beliefs and judgements held by the majority culture.

Even when multicultural education is viewed as a focus on issues — prejudice, racism, discrimination, ethnic or cultural rights, the message may be one of "you make up your own mind because your decision is as good as anyone else's", or that certain things are right or wrong because the society in which one lives has decreed them to be such. Exceptions to this are the Association for Values Education and Research (1978), and Morton & McBride (1977), both of which take the view that prejudice is irrational regardless of whether or not any particular society has decreed it to be acceptable.

The fact is that multicultural education has not focused upon the moral principles inherent in it. Programs which teach about cultures may not have the desired effects. Interventions which assume that presenting students with historical cases of discrimination against a particular group will not only lead to gains in knowledge but will also lead to sympathy for the victims are not necessarily effective (see Kehoe, 1978; Kehoe & Echols, Chapter 9).

Multicultural education must develop the modes of reasoning for arriving at rational judgments concerning how people of differing backgrounds should be treated. If the aim in Canada is to promote group understanding and a Canadian mosaic as "the most suitable means of assuring the cultural freedom of Canadians" (House of Commons Debates, 1971), then there is more to multicultural education than learning *about* culture in its various forms. The aim has to be one of developing beliefs and modes of reasoning by which we can make intelligent decisions concerning how the needs, interests, and feelings of people should be construed, and how conflicts of interest should be resolved. Because the point of these modes of reasoning is to guide conduct, multicultural education involves initiation into rational modes of conduct which must be directed toward all people. This is an ideal which will not come to fruition unless a strong educational effort is made. This effort should include the following components:

(a) The promotion of good reasoning,
(b) The development of concept of person,
(c) The development of a concept and sense of self-worth,
(d) The development of a concept of society,
(e) The understanding of such concepts as prejudice, and stereotyping.

Components of multicultural education based on moral principles

The promotion of good reasoning

Multicultural education should attempt to develop in students the ability to think critically about information with which they are presented and the ability to reason well with that information. A simple example will illustrate how these abilities can be used to arrive at a sound, defensible position on a specific issue. Alex McQuirter, head of the Ku Klux Klan in Canada, recently made a statement that "Seventy-five percent of the hand guns in Vancouver are owned by East Indians. It's important that white people begin to defend themselves." Rather than accepting McQuirter's argument at face value, it seems preferable to examine it to ascertain whether or not the fact is true and whether or not his conclusion is logically derived from his factual claim.

First, it seems reasonable to ask how many guns McQuirter is discussing, 75% of what? (of a few, or of thousands of guns?) Second, we must ask if the statement is true. McQuirter's statement is an empirical claim and its truth might be assessed by telephoning the Vancouver Police Department. In this case we were unable to ascertain the truth or falsity of this claim — the evidence was not available to us. The statement is presumably a clever piece of propaganda. Third, we must look at McQuirter's conclusion. Arguments are made up of premises which provide support for a conclusion. In order to accept McQuirter's conclusion we would have to be provided with further evidence to make the case that "whites" had to begin defending themselves. His argument, as it stands, offers only one questionable premise in support of his rather dangerous conclusion.

McQuirter's deficient argument points out the importance of being able to critically evaluate information. There are a large number of skills that can be subsumed under the term critical thinking. Evaluating McQuirter's argument required the ability to judge whether his fact was accurate and adequate to support his conclusion, whether assumptions had been made, and whether the conclusion followed logically from the premises.

Ennis (1969) defines critical thinking as "the correct assessing of statements" and identifies such specific skills as: grasping the meaning of a statement and judging (1) whether there is ambiguity in a line of reasoning; (2) whether certain statements contradict each other; (3) whether a statement is specific enough; (4) whether a statement is actually the application of a certain principle; (5) whether an observation statement is reliable; (6) whether a definition is adequate; and (7) whether a statement made by an alleged authority is acceptable. Each aspect, of course, requires teaching different things. For example, in order to judge whether a statement made by an alleged authority is acceptable, one could use Ennis' criteria of what constitutes an acceptable authority:

> "He has a good reputation; the statement is in his field; he was disinterested — that is, he did not knowingly stand to profit by the results of his statement (except that he may have stood to have his reputation affected); his reputation could be affected by

his statement and he was aware of this fact when he made his statement; he studied the matter; he followed accepted procedures in coming to his conclusion (although there are legitimate exceptions to this requirement); he was in full possession of his faculties." (1969: 393)

Critical evaluation of statements made by alleged authorities leads us to another aspect of critical thinking — recognition of informal fallacies. An argument can be fallacious in two ways: formally, that is, the conclusion does not follow logically from the premises; or informally, that is, the arguments are deceptive, either intentionally or unintentionally. Although they may contain worthwhile ideas, no evidence is provided in support of their conclusions. There are a large number of informal fallacies and not everyone classifies them in the same way or describes them by the same names. Here we will touch on only a few of the most common.

If someone suggested that it must be true that 75% of hand guns in Vancouver were owned by East Indians because they had read it in the newspaper, this person would have committed an informal fallacy. Appealing to authorities, in this case the newspaper, provides absolutely no evidence for the statement's truth or falsity. Because we have all been taught, to some degree or another, to obey and respect authority, we are reluctant to challenge what famous people say, or what long-held traditions and beliefs dictate. A well-known politician may make the argument that people from country X should no longer be permitted to immigrate to Canada. Rather than accepting the statement (an appeal to authority) we should ask him what evidence he has. If he suggests that the reason is that the majority of Canadians wish to stop immigration from country X, we cannot accept this as adequate evidence. If arguments were acceptable simply because large numbers of people believed that they were, then we would have to grant that, for a great number of years, the earth was flat because large numbers of people believed that to be true. Similarly, it is unacceptable to argue that something should take place because it always took place in the past. If such were the case, then slavery would still be a common practice in parts of the world.

The fallacy of hasty generalization is another prevalent reasoning error. While generalizations do, at times, serve very useful purposes, generalizations based on insufficient evidence obstruct critical thinking and can foster prejudicial attitudes. Thus, being able to recognize a poor generalization is a worthwhile aim for a multicultural education program, and, indeed, for any education program. Because one Japanese woman wears a kimono does not necessarily mean that all Japanese women do. This fallacy of hasty generalization is somewhat similar to the fallacy of division. Here one argues that because a group has a specific characteristic, then all members of that group also have that characteristic. For example, a teacher may tell her class that Ukrainians paint eggs at Easter time. Students may then expect every Ukrainian they meet to paint eggs. Obviously, this is poor reasoning.

If someone asserts a causal link between events when there is insufficient grounds to establish the link, then he is committing the fallacy of false cause. To say that the Ku Klux Klan is on the rise again because of a recent influx of immigrants is begging the question or circular reasoning. Here one restates one's conclusion in a different way instead of offering support for the conclusion; for example, "There has been an increased amount of racial tension in Canada in recent years because there are so many races here and none of them can get along with each other". The examples used here are obvious, but informal fallacies can be more sophisticated. It is easily understood, however, that recognition of fallacies such as these will help students avoid forming stereotypical pictures of minority groups and making ill-informed judgements about specific actions and events.

Precise use of language is another significant aspect of critical thinking (Wilson, 1966). It is very difficult to discuss anything seriously if the participants have different notions of what is being discussed. In multicultural education, there are numerous concepts which require clarification. Does "ethnic" mean membership in a group which is biologically defined, or is it based on self-identification? (Young, 1979). Concept clarification is not just a semantic game, for judgments made concerning multicultural education, or indeed anything, are based on meanings.

In addition to learning to think critically, multicultural education must include learning to reason well about value issues, particularly those in the moral domain. When making judgments concerning the needs, interests and feelings of other people, students will be better equipped if they have certain skills and abilities. Those minimally necessary for reasoning about value questions have been summarized by the Association for Values Education and Research[1] as follows:

(a) Being able to differentiate value judgements, claims, or issues from other sorts of judgments, claims, or issues.

(b) Understanding the structure or logic of value reasoning such that one can tell whether one's own and others' value arguments are sound.

(c) Understanding the significantly different kinds of rules one uses in making value judgments.

It is important to be able to differentiate factual claims from value claims because we must use different ways to assess them. Factual claims used in this context are not "facts" in the ordinary sense of the word, where it is implied that something is true. Rather, factual claims describe the nature of particular statements. There are at least two kinds of factual claims — empirical claims and analytic claims. An empirical claim is one whose truth or falsity can be determined by sensory tests — looking, listening, testing. "Toronto has many ethnic restaurants" is an empirical claim whose validity can be tested simply by looking around the city. The truth of analytic claims, on the other hand, is determined by getting clear about the meanings of the words in the statement. For example, to determine the truth of the claim, "Language and culture are inseparable" we would have to get clear about the meaning of the terms.

The truth of value claims, however, cannot be determined by either of the methods appropriate for factual claims. Value claims evaluate, positively or negatively, actions, objects, and events. It is impossible for us to assert that multiculturalism is good by doing any sensory test or by clarifying the meaning of terms. Value claims are based on rules, standards or principles and are tested through reasoning about the justifiability of our principles, and the relevance of the factual claims used to the principle to which we are appealing.

Understanding the logic of an argument is central to value reasoning. Moral arguments have the same basic form as scientific or empirical arguments. A major premise, a minor premise, and a conclusion which logically follows from these premises, together form a syllogism which, in value reasoning, is called a practical syllogism. If we take the value claim, "We ought to offer equal educational opportunity to all children", and add a factual claim, "X is a child who speaks no English", then the conclusion required to make this a valid practical syllogism is "We ought to offer equal educational opportunity to X." However, one can use exactly the same factual claim to reach the opposite conclusion if one holds a different value principle. The argument might then be as follows:

Value Premise: Children who do not speak English ought not to expect educational opportunity.
Factual Premise: X is a child who speaks no English.
Value Conclusion: We ought not to expect equal educational opportunity.

In value reasoning, it is the value premise which makes the factual claim relevant to the conclusion.

A third requirement in reasoning well about value questions is to understand that value judgments can be made from a number of points of view. Because things can have worth or value for different sorts of reasons, different sorts of justification are needed for their support. Aesthetic standards such as form, shape, colour, or beauty must be used when making judgments about works of art. The prescriptive claim that "schools should be constructed with good fire escapes", is, however, made from the health and safety point of view, applying standards more appropriate to this issue. Other points of view include the economic, the prudential, and the moral. In order to avoid the mistake of supporting a judgment made from one point of view with reasons that are suitable to another point of view, it is important to be able to distinguish them. The prudential and moral points of view are often confused. Prudential judgments are usually concerned with only one's own self-interest whereas moral judgments take into account the needs, interests, and feelings of others. Judgments concerning ethnic groups are often based on prudential reasoning. For example, it is not uncommon to hear that someone does not want members of a specific minority group living in his neighbourhood because they will lower the price of his house. Multiculturalism, however, must consider the consequences of particular actions on others, not merely the consequences to self. The moral point of view is called for whenever there is a possibility that a contemplated action will threaten the significant interests and concerns of other people (Baier, 1965).

After formulating the value judgment, verifying the factual claims, ensuring that the facts are relevant, identifying the point of view, and determining that the argument is valid, one must test the principle which ties the factual claim to the conclusion. A perfectly logical argument can be based on a principle which is unacceptable, for example:

Anyone who is different from me ought to be discriminated against.
X is different from me.
Therefore, X ought to be discriminated against.

Even principles which are deemed acceptable should be tested to ascertain whether or not there are good reasons to justify them. Note that we say *test*, not *prove*. These tests will not always guarantee "right" conclusions.

The AVER assumes that moral reasoning must be guided by at least two principles:

(a) It is not right to do X unless it is right for any person in the same situation to do X.
(b) If the consequences of everyone doing X in a given circumstance are unacceptable, then it isn't right for anyone to do X in that situation.

These principles derive from a conception of morality which claims that a moral principle is acceptable if and only if all the judgments which logically follow from it are acceptable (Singer, 1963). Such principles as impartiality, justice, and equality demand consistency. All rule out favoritism for any individual. In order to get clear about these principles and provide a framework through which people can become committed to acting on these principles, the following attainments are necessary:

The ability and inclination to put oneself imaginatively into the circumstances of another person.

The ability and inclination to imagine the consequences if everyone were to engage in a particular action.

The former of these attainments entails the ability to role-take. If one is to consider the needs and feelings of others, and if one is to consider the consequences of doing X to another person, then one must put oneself into the "shoes" of the other. If a person realizes in a case of discrimination that he would not appreciate being discriminated against because his feelings and needs were not being considered, then he is less likely to be discriminatory. This is the basis of the role exchange test and it requires more than the insider's perspective because it asks the student to do more than view a culture through the other's eyes. The role exchange test requires that the question be asked "Would it be *right* if I were in the other person's shoes to have X done to me?" To apply it well entails knowledge of what causes physical and psychological harm to people. Only if we know harm is caused by demeaning people, and excluding people from various institutions, organizations, roles, and rights, can we begin to detect morally hazardous actions.

The latter attainment requires application of the universal consequences test. In this case, we must imagine the consequences of everyone in similar circumstances engaging in the action described in the value judgment. After deciding whether to accept or reject the consequences of everyone in similar circumstances engaging in the action, a decision is made to accept or reject the value judgment. For example, if the value judgment is made that a particular minority group should be permitted to practice all its cultural beliefs and behaviours, then consistency requires that all groups should be permitted to practice all their cultural beliefs and behaviours.

A third test can be applied to determine whether we are willing to apply a value principle consistently. The new cases test is based on the idea that we can accept a principle only if we can accept all the judgments that issue from it. If the judgment is put forward that "The Ku Klux Klan should not be allowed to organize in Canada as its beliefs are too extreme" then, to be consistent, we should have to concede that any group that had extreme beliefs should not be allowed to organize in Canada. This may well include various types of religious, environmental, or political groups.

The final principle test is the subsumption test. It involves ascertaining whether or not a moral principle used in an argument follows logically from a more general principle, and determining whether this principle is acceptable. Suppose we argue that people ought to be allowed to practise a particular religion. As this principle is a judgment about a class of possible actions, we must accept the more general principle of "freedom of religion". If we cannot accept this principle in all cases then we must abandon the first principle or find a relevant difference between the first principle and the more general one. For example, we might argue that because a particular religion believes in human sacrifice, then this aspect is immoral. Then a principle such as the sacredness of human life might take precedence over the freedom of religion principle.

We believe that, if these tests are taken seriously, people will make more rational judgments concerning how, in a multicultural society, people are to be treated, and how conflicts between people are to be resolved. Using these tests will not guarantee right answers, but they will, at least, get people arguing in the right domain.

The concept of person

As human beings we share with all other humans certain needs such as food, protection from natural elements, affection, a sense of purpose in life, and social interaction. We also share similar capacities for feelings and emotions — we can be joyful, or miserable. These similarities provide the basis for the concept of "person". This is not merely a biological term, as in ordinary language; it is also a moral concept. Persons have certain fundamental rights and deserve respect because they have intrinsic worth. We must develop the idea that although people may live in different environments, have different histories and biographies and thus perceive their world in different ways, we are all, nevertheless, persons. Differences neither enhance nor diminish one's personhood. Differences are insignificant when it comes to determining who is to count as a person. The concept of person is a necessary condition of morality which is, after all, a set of principles and ways of reasoning about how persons are to be treated. It requires that *all persons* be treated equally unless there are relevant differences among the persons which justify differential treatment. This principle, which puts the burden of justification on those who would treat persons unequally, could not be formulated without a concept of person.

Although children at an early age know that people differ from tables and trees it appears from our own inquiries that not all elementary school children classify handicapped people, or very old people, or people with different coloured skin as "persons". It appears that, as these aforementioned people don't fit the child's physical concept of a person, the child is not willing to grant them equal rights. Presumably in a situation in which a child is harassing someone, he does not recognize the other's right to non-interference. The child neither understands the rules for appropriate social interaction, nor comprehends that he is responsible for appropriate social behaviour. There is a great deal of research which must be carried out before any educational program which focuses on the concept of person can be implemented. We need to know how people differ in the degree to which they understand and use the concept, and what circumstances might hinder understanding and use. We need to discover how children use the concept and how they might be helped to develop it. In effect, Canada's multicultural policy is premised on a concept of a person who has the right to maintain his or her cultural identity within a framework of basic democratic and justice principles. In other words, the moral attributes of personhood take precedence over the cultural ones — one has to recognize the rights of others. Yet, neither the cultural nor moral worth of a person can be developed unless there is a sense of self-worth.

The concept of self-worth

The sense of "self-worth" to which we refer is somewhat different from that which arises from being good at something or being popular. What we are referring to is the sense that because we are persons our needs, interests, and feelings are significant. Having a sense of self-worth is necessary both to the demanding of one's rights as a person and to fully appreciate the importance of other persons' rights. As is the case with the concept of person much more research is needed before we can proceed to design educational programs to enhance this capacity.

The concept of society

We all live in groups, some of which we can freely opt into and out of, others of which we do not initially choose to join, that is, the society into which we are born. Any society, be it formal or informal, has written or unwritten rules or codes, some of which are based on moral principles. In order to understand a society, or, even an organization, institution, or culture, we have, at least, to examine the bases on which it is organized and operated, the rights granted its members, and the responsibilities and duties required of its members. However, it is not enough merely to examine these bases; evaluation must also occur. A society may have a strong sense of interdependence in which all members contribute to the perceived good of the society, but still may not accord certain rights to all its members.

Concepts of prejudice and stereotyping

"Prejudice" is an ambiguous word. Denotatively, it means to prejudge, or to have prejudged; in other words an evaluation is made without regard to the facts of the particular case. In multicultural education the word is used to refer to a relatively long lasting state or condition which involves other people. We talk about being prejudiced towards minorities, or being prejudiced against a particular minority group. Prejudice is usually seen as negative because it often leads to harmful action against others. However, prejudice can lead to beneficial actions, for example, being prejudiced toward orphans or the poor and devoting time, energy, and money to their welfare. Here we will focus on the negative consequences, derogatory stereotypes and hostility or fear.

People become prejudiced in two major ways — through stereotyping and through indoctrination. Stereotyping consists of generalizing from one example to all other similar examples. For example, if person Y does something which is harmful, or has a characteristic which is viewed negatively, then stereotyping would lead one to conclude that the group to which person Y belongs shares the same characteristic and behaviour.

A second major way of becoming prejudiced is through indoctrination. In this case one is told what to believe, with no good or adequate reasons being given as to why one should accept what one is told; and questioning of any belief is discouraged. Sometimes this indoctrination is blatant, as in the case of Nazi Germany where people were explicitly and repeatedly told that certain people were inferior. But more often indoctrination is hidden and subtle. If one is socialized in a milieu in which certain people are perceived to be inferior or dangerous, then one adopts this position unthinkingly and by accident. If this is coupled with stereotyping then the prejudice can become deeply ingrained.

Both of these aspects — stereotyping and indoctrination — are irrational. They are irrational because the beliefs and actions stemming from them rely on illogical reasoning, on choosing X over Y without there being relevant differences. If X and Y were identical in every respect, and we stated that X was good and Y bad, then people would either think we were mad, or would think we knew something about X and Y which they didn't. When we choose something, people expect us to have relevant reasons for our choices.

A major concern with prejudiced behaviour is that action is based on irrelevant differences. Suppose a school baseball coach is looking for players who can throw, hit, and pitch well. Suppose also that the coach is prejudiced against people with certain facial features. The coach believes that these students are uncooperative, lazy, unreliable, and physically weak. When the coach first meets the team applicants, he assumes that anyone from this group has all the negative qualities of the stereotype. This leads to a negative attitude toward this student and a disinclination to accord him a fair chance at playing baseball. This is unreasonable because facial features are not an indicator of co-operativeness, reliability or physical strength. The reasoning is based on irrelevant differences and can lead to imprudent and immoral actions.

It is likely that we are all prejudiced and ordinarily we ought not to be blamed for being prejudiced. If you meet a person who on two occasions has treated you disrespectfully, you are likely to avoid contact with that person on the third occasion even though you have prejudged — you don't know that the person will treat you badly on the third occasion. However, you cannot assume that other similar people will treat you badly. Therefore, we have to learn what prejudice is, what our prejudices are, why prejudice is irrational and under what circumstances it is likely to be immoral. In this volume, Kehoe & Echols (Chapter 9) present theoretical perspectives and educational approaches for combatting racism and stereotyping in the schools.

Conclusions

This paper has placed multicultural education into a moral framework. It has been argued that the majority of current approaches to multiculturalism are inadequate. If schools are to respond in an educationally defensible manner to the needs of a multicultural society, then the moral point of view must be taken. This moral point of view entails a rejection of ethical relativism and a commitment to cultural relativism. When these two constructs come into conflict a variety of concepts, skills, dispositions and sensitivities are necessary to arrive at morally justifiable resolutions. It has been concluded that at least the following attainments will be necessary to make rational decisions:

(a) The ability to think critically.
(b) The ability to reason well about moral issues.
(c) The development of concepts such as person, self-worth, prejudice, and stereotyping.

Although much research of an empirical and conceptual nature remains to be done on sections of this final attainment, the first two are sufficiently clear to warrant immediate inclusion in curriculum materials. We cannot address the fundamental question of multiculturalism — how should people be treated? — without consideration of the moral domain, for the moral domain is concerned with how the needs, interests, and feelings of people are to be considered, and how conflicts between people are to be resolved.

Note to Chapter Eight

1. The Association for Values Education and Research (AVER) is an unincorporated body of professors and graduate students in the Faculty of Education at the University of British Columbia. Since 1970, the AVER has been studying two problems: what it means to be morally educated, and how best to educate people in the domain of morality.

References

ASSOCIATION FOR VALUES EDUCATION AND RESEARCH. 1978, *Prejudice*. Toronto: Ontario Institute for Studies in Education.

BAIER, K. 1965, *The Moral point of view*. New York: Random House.

BURKE, M. 1978, *Ukrainian Canadians*. Toronto: Van Nostrand Reinhold.

ENNIS, R. 1969, *Logic in Teaching*. Englewood Cliffs, N.J.: Prentice-Hall.

HARE,. R. 1952, *The language of morals*. London: Oxford University Press.

HOUSE OF COMMONS DEBATES. 1971, Ottawa: Government of Canada. October 8.

ITO, R. 1978, *The Japanese Canadians*. Toronto: Van Nostrand Reinhold.

JOHNSON, R. & BLAIR, J. 1980, *Informal logic*. California: Edgepress.

KEHOE, J. 1978, *Ethnic prejudice and the role of the school*. Vancouver: University of British Columbia.

MASTRANGELO, R. 1979, *The Italian Canadians*. Toronto: Van Nostrand Reinhold.

MORTON, T. & MCBRIDE, J. 1977, *Look again: The process of prejudice and discrimination*. Vancouver: Concept Publishing.

PETERS, R. 1966, *Ethics and education*. London: Allen & Unwin.

SINGER, M. 1963, *Generalization in ethics*. London: Eyre & Spottiswoode.

TORNEY, J. 1977, The international attitudes and knowledge of adolescents in nine countries: The IEA Cure Education Survey. *International Journal of Political Education*, 1, 3–20.

TRAVIS, C. 1974, What does college do for a person; frankly very little: An interview with Theodore Newcomb. *Psychology Today*, 8.

WERNER, W. 1981, The illusion of neutrality. *Horizon*, 19 (3), 40–42.

WILLIAMS, D. & SALYACHIVIN, S. 1973, A re-investigation of strategies for the teaching of international understanding. Vancouver: Educational Research Institute of B.C. April.

WILSON, J. 1966, *Thinking with concepts*. Cambridge: Cambridge University Press.

WOOD, D. & REMNANT, R. 1980, *The people we are*. Toronto: Gage.

WRIGHT, I. & COOMBS, J. 1981, *The cogency of multiculturalism*. Occasional Papers Series. Vancouver: University of British Columbia, Centre for the Study of Curriculum and Instruction.

YOUNG, J. C. 1979, Education in a multicultural society: What sort of education? What sort of society? *Canadian Journal of Education*, 4 (3), 5–21.

9 Educational approaches for combatting prejudice and racism

John Kehoe and Frank Echols
University of British Columbia

Abstract. Several theoretical perspectives about combatting prejudicial attitudes are reviewed within the context of what is possible in schools. It is also argued that change must take place at various levels and a particular strategem is presented.

An essential component of any multicultural education program is the development of strategies to reduce prejudicial attitudes and discriminatory behaviour. A prejudiced person is not likely to be amenable to various manifestations of multiculturalism in Canadian society (see Wright & LaBar, Chapter 8). In recent years hundreds of programs have been devised to reduce prejudice. Unfortunately many of the programs lend credence to the claim that the history of education is a history of untested assumptions. Teachers develop strategies with the explicit intention of transmitting information but with the implicit assumption of improving understanding or appreciation. When pressed, teachers will concede the latter to mean "liking" or "acceptance" although they are reluctant to do so because it suggests indoctrination. Teachers provide information about cultures by using textbooks, showing pictures, filmstrips, and films; and by having students do "projects" using library books. The implicit and untested assumption is that these experiences will develop more positive attitudes toward culturally diverse groups. But the intended outcome may not be achieved and there may well be unanticipated outcomes — including negative effects (see Connors, Chapter 7; Wyatt, Chapter 6). In addition to unwarranted assumptions Buchignani (1982) has observed that most programs used so far are

130

isolated interventions and no such single project can have much effect in a milieu which contradicts its spirit.

There is the further difficulty of unpredictable strategies. Strategies sometimes work with one teacher in one situation but not with another or in a different situation. The likelihood of developing programs which are effective increases if they are based on sound theoretical considerations and provision is made for systematic evaluation of the effects.

There is general agreement among social scientists that prejudice is a learned phenomenon. Discriminatory behaviour is held to be undesirable in Canadian society, as it is inconsistent with widely accepted beliefs in the dignity of humankind and human rights (Wright & LaBar, Chapter 8). Strategies directed toward the reduction of prejudice and concomitant discrimination should focus on presumed causes of prejudice.

There are several theoretical perspectives to which policy makers could look for guidance in developing programs to reduce prejudice and increase acceptance of multiculturalism. For example, Patel (1980) identified personality attributes, social forces and institutions as sources of prejudice. McLemore (1980) included: socialization into a group or culture of which prejudice is a part (cultural transmission theory); psychological development of personality in which the individual "benefits" from prejudicial attitudes in that it is compatible with some personality "needs" (personality theory); economic benefits of majority groups from minority group discrimination (group gain theory); and the development of ethnocentric group solidarity which leads to "in-group" and "out-group" categorizations (group identification theory). The role of the school in reducing prejudice caused by these various sources is more apparent for some than for other theoretical perspectives.

Prejudiced personality

The prejudiced personality perspective has two major theoretical orientations. The first views prejudice as an outgrowth of psychological conflict and associated defence mechanisms and the second emphasizes underdeveloped cognitive-perceptual mechanisms. An example of the former is ego-defensiveness and the resulting need for scapegoating. A person may be prejudiced because he perceives himself to be a failure. He cannot blame himself and must find someone else to blame. Ego-defensiveness is frequently put forward as a cause of prejudice toward such perceived high achievers as Chinese and Jewish students. Students hold the prejudices because they believe Jewish or Chinese students are causing them to be less successful by studying all the time and raising the standards. These students are not conforming to the norms of avoiding school work and having fun. In order to defend their ego they blame the Chinese students for their lack of success. Katz, Sarnoff & McClintock (1956) successfully reduced ego-defensiveness by inducing self-insight. Students read a description of the phenomenon and then read a case history of someone like themselves holding prejudices for those reasons. It would seem apparent that the first task is to determine whether ego-defensiveness is a cause of prejudice among students. Yau (1981) was surprised to find little evidence of prejudice caused by a need for ego-defensiveness among a small group of Catholic high school students in Metro Toronto. If it is found that most high school students do not manifest ego-defensiveness as a cause of prejudice then it may not be appropriate to design programs to reduce ego-defensiveness. Although a program designed to "innoculate" students against having a need for ego-defensiveness in the future could be a possibility.

The second theoretical orientation within the prejudiced personality refers to underdeveloped cognitive-perceptual abilities. The phenomena associated with intergroup perception can be adequately accounted for as natural consequences of more general cognitive processes by which human beings structure, simplify, and give meaning to their social environment. Hohn (1973) trained kindergarten children in logical thinking tasks designed to enhance perspective taking ability. Preoperational children operate from their own point of view and are generally unaware of the viewpoint or perspective of others. Once distinctions can be made between their own perspective and the perspective of others, the children become conscious of their own viewpoints as particular ones. Perceptual activity of a visual and tactile nature facilitates the acquisition of spatial perspective. Hohn's training program included tasks involving conservation of quantity, subordinate classification, reversibility, multiple relations and two and three dimensional perspective training. An example of a perspective taking task is to place two feather dusters on the centre of the table so that the plumes face one pupil but not the others in a small group. The pupils are first asked to mark on their sheets, the position of the dusters as they see them. They are then asked to indicate the dusters as the one pupil would see them. As much as possible the children are to assist one another in developing an understanding that a different viewpoint depends on one's location.

Hohn found that the training on Piagetian tasks resulted in significant improvement in pupil ability to perform the tasks and a significant decline in pro-white bias in selecting pictures. Gibson (1982) replicated the study with some modifications. She found that experimental subjects performed significantly better on the Piagetian tasks but did not have less pro-white bias when compared with control subjects. The measure of pro-white bias had thirty-two such items such as, "Two girls owned a dog. One was kind to the *dog*. Which one was kind?" In the Hohn study subjects were given a choice of a black girl and a white girl. In the Gibson study the pictures were of the same girl but the skin tone of one was black and the other was white. In the Gibson study each training session lasted for one half hour which was fifteen minutes shorter than Hohn's training sessions. The change in ability to do the Piagetian tasks was enough to reach statistical significance, but may not have been sufficient to effect pro-white bias.

Katz (1976) has investigated the importance of perception within cognitive perceptual theory. She found that highly prejudiced children judge faces of another race as considerably more similar than do children who are low in prejudice. Similarly prejudiced children tend to use a small number of colour cues to label members of a group which increases their perception of intragroup similarity. Prejudice was reduced by teaching children to associate names to faces and to look for cues other than skin colour to judge ways in which faces from within a racial group were the same and different from one another. The association of distinctive names with people and the use of cues other than skin colour to differentiate people within a group reduced prejudice. Katz's research emphasizes the importance of textbook and curricular reform which would introduce members of many racial groups as distinct human beings with similar needs, strengths and weaknesses as the pupils.

There are other approaches to attitude and behavioural change which have demonstrated their effectiveness, at least in the short run, and are somewhat consistent with the theoretical orientations already described. Kehoe (1980) described how curriculum materials should emphasize good news and accentuate similarities between cultures. Appeals to consistency have been effective. Demonstrating inconsistencies between values, such as equality and prejudice, may change attitudes. The application of tests of principles: role exchange, new cases, subsumption and universalization to cases, may change attitudes. Using cases to appeal to sympathy, appropriate use of personal contact, reinforcement, role playing and simulations have all been effective in changing attitudes in some situations. Buchignani (1982) has added direct modification of behaviour to this list. He points out that most projects are oriented to changing prejudices in order to eliminate discrimination and there is considerable support for using the opposite approach. If people are required to act equally, many will eventually come to think equally.

Social forces and group gains theories

The social forces perspective sees prejudice as caused by economic cycles and the competitive nature of the political economy. The majority benefit economically from minority group discrimination. The obvious solution is far reaching socio-economic reform (Reitz, 1982) but the role of the school in achieving that goal is less obvious. One response of the school has been to have students read and discuss historical and contemporary cases of discrimination. The relationship between majority group gains and minority groups as victims is presented to the students. It is assumed that knowledge will mean that as future citizens and policy makers they would advocate fundamental reform of the political economy and thus reduce prejudice and discrimination. A more detailed look at the assumption teachers make when they use such an approach suggests the following:

(a) Teaching students to recognize instances of prejudice and discrimination and their unacceptability suggests that the school is attempting to transmit a different set of beliefs than those which may be held by various groups in society.

(b) The presentation of injustice in the past will make a significant contribution to the development of a concept of justice.

(c) The presentation of cases of discrimination will make a significant contribution to the feelings of sympathy for the victims.

(d) A review of courses of study shows considerable emphasis on teaching the commonality of humankind. When cases of discrimination are presented the students could identify with the victims and perceive them as part of their ingroup.

(e) Students will evaluate the victims of discrimination positively and the perpetrators of the injustice negatively. Kehoe & Echols (1982) attempted to test some of these assumptions. Secondary students were presented with print materials describing various forms of discrimination. Eight incidents involving discrimination in Canada's past were selected. They included discrimination toward Canadians of Jewish, West Indian, Native Indian, Chinese, Japanese, and East Indian origin. Two short examples of the material used are:

    (i) Williams Lake, British Columbia, 1966, an Indian girl met some youths in a beverage room, and they agreed to give her a lift to her aunt's place. Of course, they didn't take her to her aunt's; they took her to a garbage dump, where the three whites thought they would get a little free loving. Everybody knows about Indian girls.

Unfortunately this girl didn't. She was found dead the next morning, naked and dead by the roadside. The youths, all of good families, admitted that they had wrestled her around some, got fed up with her, and pitched her out of the car into the cold April night.

She died of a broken neck, but they said she was alive when they last saw her. What they did wasn't right maybe, but it wasn't murder either. A white jury agreed; two of the youths were convicted of assault and fined $200; the charge against the third was dismissed. (Stewart, 1976: 1)

(ii) The war with Japan brought the prejudice to the surface. On the day Pearl Harbour was attacked, a young Vancouver girl named Yoshiko Kurita was walking home when an old man came up and spat in her face. That afternoon when Yoshiko's mother boarded a streetcar, a white passenger tore off her hat and stamped on it. (Patton, 1973: 19–20)

As a result of the treatment, experimental subjects did not show a significant decrease in their feeling of social distance toward minority groups mentioned in the treatment which suggests that the presentation of the cases did not cause them to perceive the minorities as more a part of their ingroup than they had before. Nor did the experimental subjects show more concern, shock or anger about what had happened. The presentation of cases of discrimination did not result in increased sympathy for victims. An examination of the absolute scores for both experimental and control groups showed lower social distance and more sympathy for Chinese and Japanese victims than for East Indians. British Columbia subjects are more familiar with Chinese and Japanese people and consider them "old" immigrants as compared to East Indians.

These results can be explained, in part, by an examination of Hornstein's we–they theory and Lerner's (1980) belief in a just world theory. Hornstein, Mason, Solek & Heilman (1971) attempted to identify conditions which affect an individual's disposition to behave altruistically. They found opinion similarity to be related to helpful behaviour. Holloway, Tucker & Hornstein (1976) investigated the effects of good and bad news on the altruism of subjects. Good news promoted altruistic behaviour. They suggested that bad news adversely affects a "we-feeling" and tends to weaken social bonds. The former study provides support for the argument that defining others as similar to ourselves is an important aspect of the classroom methodology for promoting positive attitudes towards minorities.

Studies done with the British Columbia population indicate that the white groups consider the Japanese and Chinese to have similar belief systems to their own and East Indians to have dissimilar belief systems (Berry, Kalin & Taylor, 1977). The latter studies provide support for the argument that too much emphasis on bad news will result in a minority group being defined as an "outgroup". There has been much publicity of incidents of racism toward East Indians and as a result they are defined as a "they" or an outgroup.

Lerner (1980) has postulated a theory of the existence of a belief in a just world. He points out that when people are confronted with an instance of undeserved suffering, they have at least two alternatives. They could accept the situation at face value as unjust and react with indignation, fear and compassion for the victims. The majority of people, however, seem to elect the alternative of re-establishing justice in their world by deciding that the victim was a relatively "inferior" person who happened to be suffering for a good cause. Once people know someone's fate, they will be inclined to construe the value of that person and the value of their efforts to fit that fate. It may be that much teaching, which has the implicit intention of causing students to react positively to historical and contemporary victims, in fact causes them to react negatively and to denigrate the victims. Lerner also found that when subjects identify with the victims, less derogation of the victim is the result. Identifying with the victim is important because the norm of helping those with whom you identify is strongly held. One of the results of the Kehoe & Echols' study was that subjects concluded that acts of discrimination were frequent occurrences when the victims were Japanese and Chinese but not frequent when the victims were East Indian. The results suggest that subjects define acts of discrimination against Chinese and Japanese as discrimination because the Chinese and Japanese have been here for a relatively long period of time and are considered part of the ingroup. They are therefore entitled to fair treatment which they did not receive. East Indians are an outgroup and therefore unacceptable as victims of discrimination in a just society. They are perceived to have been here for a relatively short period of time, they are an outgroup and therefore not entitled to fair treatment. The results of this study are not an argument for abandoning the teaching of historical and contemporary cases of discrimination. They do, however, suggest the need for testing alternative methodologies for ensuring the achievement of the assumptions made by teachers.

Institutional prejudice

This perspective sees prejudice as caused by the norms of institutions (D'Oyley, 1982). An adequately qualified person from another culture may be rejected as an employee because: they might not fit in, customers might be offended by different politeness systems, they might take over, they don't have Canadian experience. Two recent studies (Ramsay, Sneddon, Grenfell & Ford, 1982; Perry, Clifton & Hryniuk, 1981) found that schools with the lowest levels of truancy, vandalism, anti-social behaviour and the potential for higher levels of achievement were those with a clearly articulated multicultural philosophy in the school. The teachers modified their textbooks, altered their teaching styles, had high pupil expectations, and made every effort to avoid offending their students. They did not blame the students for failure but rather looked to themselves and their programs. The emphasis was on praise for good behaviour and deeds rather than punishment for misbehaviour. On the other hand the schools which operationalized an assimilationist philosophy had in addition to poorer performance on the variables already described, ethnic gangs, teams selected on the basis of race and more negative stereotyping. Perry *et al.* (1981) examined three schools and found that students had more positive attitudes when the school emphasized multiculturalism in all aspects of schooling.

A particular strategem and conclusions

It may be that reform of the structure and climate of the school is more important than developing personality attributes as a means of reducing prejudice. To that end a non-profit society in British Columbia, *Alternatives to Racism*[1], has prepared *A Handbook of Selected Activities for Enhancing the Multicultural Climate of the School*. The *Handbook* makes practical suggestions for: justifying multicultural education; responding to prejudiced opinions stated as facts; increasing community participation; assessing the multicultural climate of the school; revising the hidden curriculum of the school so that recognition is given to minority cultures; and making accommodations to persistent areas of culture especially in the realm of verbal and non-verbal behaviour. In addition the *Handbook* makes suggestions for the examination of textbooks for bias. A conceptual framework for curriculum development is provided which points out the differences between prejudiced and unprejudiced children and makes suggestions of activities which if incorporated in the existing curriculum could enhance the cognitive-perceptual abilities, role taking abilities and the self-esteem of students. The intent is to reduce "student to student" prejudice. Finally, the *Handbook* makes recommendations for assessment for placement. The point is made that even if assessment procedures are made more fair the unfairness will be perpetuated unless program reform takes place which recognizes and makes accommodation to the cultures represented in the school.

This paper has argued that change must take place at many levels. One should also look to a number of theoretical orientations for assistance in developing policy and programs. Changes must be made in the curriculum especially to activities which influence student attitudes toward each other. Changes need to be made in the regulations and aspects of schooling which assume that all students are from an Anglo-Christian heritage and with the school setting out to assimilate the others. Finally changes need to be made in the structures of institutions other than schools so they behave more accommodatingly to cultural diversity. Schools may have more leverage to bring about changes within their own functions. They are not, however, set up to change their own basic organization. However, as Ogbu (1978) has suggested, by teaching that social rewards should be distributed on the basis of ability, minorities become more aware of the unfairness of job ceilings and begin to make demands on institutions. Alterations in the basic character of institutions themselves may only come with a new framework such as that discussed by D'Oyley (Chapter 11).

References

BERRY, J. W. KALIN, R. & TAYLOR, D. M. 1977, *Multiculturalism and ethnic attitudes in Canada*. Ottawa: Supply and Services Canada.

BUCHIGNANI, N. 1982, Practical strategies to foster inter-racial harmony through the educational system. In V. D'OYLEY (ed.), *Perspectives on race, education and social development: Emphasis on Canada*. Vancouver: University of British Columbia, Centre for the Study of Curriculum and Instruction.

D'OYLEY, V. 1982, *Perspectives on race, education and social development: Emphasis on Canada*. Vancouver: University of British Columbia, Centre for the Study of Curriculum and Instruction.

GIBSON, J. 1982, Effects of perceptual training on racial preference of kindergarten children. Vancouver: University of British Columbia.

HOHN, R. L. 1973, Perceptual training and its effect on racial preferences of kindergarten children. *Psychological Reports*, 32, 435–41.

HORNSTEIN, H. A., MASON, H. N., SOLEK, A. & HEILMAN, M. 1971, Effects of sentiment and completion of a helping act on observer helping: A case for socially mediated Zeignarnick effects. *Journal of Personality and Social Psychology*, 1, 107–12.

HOLLOWAY, S., TUCKER, L. & HORNSTEIN, H. A. 1976, The effects of social and non-social information on interpersonal behaviour: The news makes news. Columbia University, Teachers College.

KATZ, P. 1976, The acquisition of racial attitudes in children. In P. A. KATZ (ed.), *Towards the elimination of racism*. Elmsford, New York: Pergamon Press.

KATZ, D., SARNOFF, J. & McCLINTOCK, C. 1956, Ego-defense and attitude change. *Human Relations*, 9, 27–45.

KEHOE, J. 1980, Achieving cultural diversity in Canadian schools. Cornwall, Ontario, Vesta.

KEHOE, JOHN W. 1984, *A Handbook for enhancing the multicultural climate of the school*. University of British Columbia: Western Education Development Group.

KEHOE, J. & ECHOLS, F. 1983, The effects of reading historical and contemporary cases of discrimination on attitudes toward selected minority groups. *Ethnic Studies*, xv, 2, 92–106.

LERNER, M. J. 1980, *The belief in a just world*. New York: Plenum Press.

McLEMORE, D. S. 1980, *Racial and ethnic relations in America*. Toronto: Allyn & Bacon.

OGBU, J. U. 1978, *Minority education and caste*. New York: Academic Press.

PATEL, D. 1980, *Dealing with interracial conflict: Policy alternatives*. Montreal: The Institute for Research on Public Policy.

PATTON, J. 1973, *The exodus of the Japanese*. Toronto: McClelland & Stewart.

PERRY, R., CCLIFTON, R. & HRYNIUK, S. 1981, *Multiculturalism in Winnipeg schools: A preliminary analysis of selected student, teacher, and school characteristics*. Winnipeg: Canadian Council of Christians and Jews.

RAMSAY, P., SNEDDON, D., GRENFELL, J. & FORD, T. 1982, *Tomorrow it may be too late*. Hamilton, New Zealand: University of Waikato.

REITZ, J. 1982, Race relations in the contemporary Canadian labour market: A discussion of research and policy. In V. D'OYLEY (ed.), *Perspectives on race, education and social development: Emphasis on Canada*. Vancouver: University of British Columbia, Centre for the Study of Curriculum and Instruction.

STEWART, W. 1976, *But not in Canada*. Toronto: Macmillan.

YAU, M. 1981, *How to change anti-Chinese attitudes among high school students*. Toronto: The Ontario Institute for Studies in Education.

Future Directions for
Educational Policy

10 The future of language policy in education

G. Richard Tucker
Center for Applied Linguistics

Abstract. This chapter considers seven questions regarding educational policy with the aim to understand the Canadian position in relationship to those of other countries (specific examples are chosen from the Cameroons, Ecuador, Jordan, Nigeria, the People's Republic of China, and the United States). A series of predictions are made concerning directions for Canada's educational language policy. The paper concludes by suggesting that the Canadian situation is not at all unique and that educational planners should seek advice, consultation, and assistance from others, particularly those working in developing countries.

Educators, in diverse countries, have for millenia been faced with the necessity of teaching some of their pupils via a "weaker" language (see Cummins, Chapter 5; Engle, 1975; Lewis, 1976; Mackey, 1967). This situation has arisen in countries where some foreign language of wider communication (e.g. English, French) or an indigenous national language (e.g. Amharic, Pilipino, Swahili) has been adopted as a medium of instruction for all pupils; or in a country where immigrant children from diverse backgrounds enter a monolingual school system (e.g. Chicano or Portuguese youngsters in the United States; Ukrainian or German youngsters in several of the western provinces of Canada); or perhaps even in a setting where speakers of a non-standard variety (e.g. Haitian Creole, Cape Verdian Criulo) attend a school where the teachers and the texts employ only a more prestigious standard form. Faced with situations such as these, many educators have adopted some form of second language or bilingual instruction.

Recently, programs of bilingual instruction have been implemented in numerous developing countries where the following conditions apply: (a) there is an attempt to introduce universal primary (and, in some countries,

143

secondary) education, despite a paucity of trained teachers, texts and build-ings; (b) there exists a growing concern with the validity of educational goals developed by colonial powers which reflected the values, attitudes and needs of metropolitan Paris or London; (c) there exists a desire to develop permanent functional literacy for the greatest possible number of citizens; and (d) there exists an increasingly strong belief that language can serve as a vehicle to foster a sense of self-esteem, ethnic awareness, identity or pride (e.g. Alatis, 1978; Brann, 1978; Dutcher, 1982; Hartford, Valdman & Foster, 1982; Richmond, 1982; Tucker, 1977).

Finally, of course, programs of bilingual instruction have been imple-mented in many countries where a serious desire exists to develop pupils' competence in each of two official languages (e.g. Flemish and French in parts of Belgium; English and French in parts of Canada; Afrikaans and English in parts of South Africa). In general, bilingual education programs are designed to achieve one of two basic goals. Some are clearly formulated to foster or to maintain equal facility in both languages with a concomitant development of appreciation for the values and traditions of both ethno-linguistic groups, while others use the development of early skills in the child's mother tongue as a "bridge" leading toward a more effective develop-ment of ability in some other target language (see Cummins, Chapter 5).

Questions regarding educational policy

Is it possible to speak about a "Canadian approach" to bilingual educa-tion? Are the experiences of educators in other countries relevant when it comes to charting directions for future educational policy in Canada? It has been argued elsewhere (Tucker, 1977) that the selection of a language or languages to be taught or to be used for instruction clearly contributes an important aspect of educational and of national planning.

A series of questions regarding educational policy is first considered. The aim is to understand the Canadian position with respect to each ques-tion in relationship to those of other countries and finally to make some generalizations about probable future directions for educational policy in Canada.

1. Does the country have an official federal language policy? Does that policy govern the selection of language(s) of instruction in public education?

2. Does the country have complementary or conflicting federal and provincial language policies?

3. Is the population of the country relatively homogeneous by mother tongue and ethnic origin? If not, do there exist sizable ethnolinguistic groups

within the polity who are cohesive and who have managed to achieve economic or political power? Have any or all of these diverse ethnolinguistic groups been "recognized" and accorded any special rights and treatment?

4. Does the country have a federally controlled or administered system of public education? What is the role or place of second language teaching in formal education?

5. If "responsibility" for public education rests with the provincial government, does the federal government nonetheless influence educational policy by the way it allocates supplemental funding?

6. What expectations exist concerning the role that parents, peers, and other extracurricular or societal sources will play in the lifelong education of an individual? How specific are the curricular goals that are established within the formal educational system? What direct role, if any, do parents play in shaping educational policy? How is accomplishment or competency typically assessed?

7. What research evidence exists to support claims for the differential efficacy of various pedagogical approaches?

Because it is often easier to bring a familiar situation into sharper focus by means of comparison and contrast, information about the role of *language* in education is presented from the Cameroons, Ecuador, Jordan, Nigeria, the People's Republic of China (PRC) and the United States. These examples have been specifically chosen because the educational traditions and language context of each are quite different. Each of these is considered before attempting to profile the Canadian situation.

The role of language in education in other countries

The Cameroons

The Cameroons, like Canada, is a bilingual country. English and French have been designated as the two official languages. Unlike Canada where sizable groups of individuals speak English or French as their mother tongues the majority of Cameroonians speak one of several hundred indigenous languages (Sociolinguistic Survey Team, 1979). In the Cameroons, there are separate English medium and French medium school systems. Language policy is set by the federal, not by the provincial, government. Responsibility for formal education rests within the federal government which prescribes curricula and textbooks, and sets school-leaving examinations. In the English sector, French is taught formally as a second language and vice versa. As mentioned previously, the population of the country is extremely heterogeneous by mother tongue. Although several sizable groups exist (e.g. Ewondo, Fulfulde, Bafoussan), they have not yet emerged as ethnic "pressure groups" in the same way that we think of such groups in North America. None have been accorded special status with respect to the role of language in education. At the present time, a number of pilot or experimental projects (such as PROPELCA — Programme de recherche opérationelle sur l'enseignement des langues des Cameroons) are underway. They take as their goal the development of curricula and materials and the training of teachers in a large number of indigenous languages so that schooling in the early primary years can be conducted in local languages. The long-term trend is very definitely toward the use of local languages in formal education, at least in the early primary grades. At the present time, the learning of English or French is for the most part synonymous with access to and continued participation in formal education and most graduates of secondary education are able to enter English-medium or French-medium tertiary level programs and compete on an equal footing with Anglophones or Francophones. Parents in the Cameroons, Jordan, Nigeria and the PRC play a less prominent role in shaping educational policy than do their western counterparts.

Ecuador

The official language of Ecuador, one of the smallest countries of South America, is Spanish. However, approximately two million of the country's estimated seven and a half million residents speak Quechua. In addition there are a number of other separate indigenous non-Spanish languages spoken natively in Ecuador; and up to nine distinct, well described dialects of Quechua are spoken. The language situation is one of diglossia with Spanish being the language of higher ascribed economic or social status. The government groups more than 700 separate Indian groups together for purposes of legislation and aid, but most of Ecuador's indigenous population does not acknowledge a broad ethnic identity. The federal constitution of 1945 mandated a public educational system with education, a function of the state, to be free, non-religious and obligatory. The constitution also prescribes that Quechua should be the medium of instruction in those areas of the country where it is the primary medium of communication. In fact, for many years the Ecuadorean educational system was essentially a monolingual Spanish system which consisted of a basic 6-year compulsory cycle followed by a 3-year post-primary cycle and three more years of technical or academic training. Allocation of educational resources has been uneven and the rural areas particularly neglected. During the past 15 years, increasing attention has been paid to the development of bilingual education programs in rural areas. The implementation of bilingual programs has been slow because the large majority of primary teachers are monolingual speakers of Spanish.

In 1979 the federal Department of Education proposed a concerted effort to create an awareness of the value of the Quechua language and culture. This program of sensitizing individuals to the values, attitudes, and traditions of the Quechua people is extremely important since, in many cases, parents have resisted Quechua language instruction on the belief that this would serve to further isolate their youngsters from participating in the economic development of Ecuador.

Jordan

The Hashemite Kingdom of Jordan is officially an Arabic-speaking country. Formal education at the primary and secondary levels is conducted exclusively via Arabic and by historical coincidence English is the compulsory foreign language which is studied by all students for eight years (Harrison, Prator & Tucker, 1975). Ninety-eight percent of the citizens are Arabic-speaking and there are no sizable ethnolinguistic minority groups. The public educational system is centrally controlled and the national Ministry of Education prescribes curricula, selects textbooks, and sets the school-leaving examinations. It is expected that students who complete their formal education will be literate and fluent in Arabic, and that they will be able to enter directly into English-medium tertiary programs such as those in the Faculty of Science at Jordan University. This latter expectation is often not realized and many students must take intensive English language training before beginning such study. To date, despite a number of suggestions concerning possible innovative programs, no research has been conducted involving the use of English to teach content material at the secondary level.

Nigeria

Nigeria, a country of widespread ethnolinguistic diversity, has adopted English as the country's official language. Education, in theory, begins in the prevailing vernacular language of the region and continues through the third primary grade with English taught as a second language. English becomes the medium of instruction from grade four onward. Language policy for the country is formulated at the federal level. Recently a "three-language formula" has been promulgated for the Federal Republic of Nigeria (1977). Under this policy, children begin their formal education in the local vernacular language (curricula, materials, and texts seem readily available for teaching via Hausa, Igbo and Yoruba; materials for at least the first primary grade level have also been developed for a number of indigenous languages). Education continues through primary three, or in some states, primary six, in the vernacular. English is taught as a second language throughout the primary cycle and is introduced as the principal medium of instruction, depending upon state policy, at either primary four or secondary one. In addition, at the secondary level, each child is expected to study one other major Nigerian language. A good deal of state autonomy exists in education although federal funding is important, particularly to offset the expenses associated with the continuing implementation of universal primary education. There do exist ethnolinguistic or tribal rivalries within Nigeria, particuarly among, but not restricted to, the Hausa, Igbo and Yoruba. The choice of English as a medium of education serves in some measure to neutralize these rivalries while simultaneously providing direct access to scientific and technological knowledge. Training in English, the official language, is regarded largely as the purview of the school, while parents and peers have traditionally been responsible for passing on the indigenous oral and cultural tribal traditions. In the past decade, a great deal of work has been done to develop more relevant primary curricula which attempt to reflect local, rather than British, values, attitudes, and traditions. Rigorous school-leaving examinations are administered to secondary school graduates, and successful candidates are, for the most part, able to compete successfully with other English-trained students at the tertiary level.

People's Republic of China (PRC)

The Mandarin "dialect" of Chinese is the official language of the PRC. Instruction for children at all levels, except in the autonomous regions such as Uighar, Inner Mongolia, and Tibet, occurs via Chinese. Children are instructed using *putonghua* the so-called "common language". Furthermore, they are introduced to literacy training using *pinyin* and then gradually "bridged" into reading with simplified characters. The country has a national curriculum for primary and middle (our secondary) schools with unified textbooks. There are bureaus of education and of higher education in each of the provinces but their major task is apparently to implement national policy. Under the Chinese constitution, the national autonomous regions are guaranteed certain language rights and are encouraged to use the indigenous languages for purposes of primary education, and local government. In effect, there appear to exist transitional bilingual education programs in the various autonomous regions. Foreign language study in the PRC is compulsory beginning with the third grade of primary school. English is now the most widely taught foreign language. Russian is rapidly declining in popularity.

The Chinese have decided, as a matter of policy, that facility in a foreign language will be an indispensable tool in their pursuit of the "four modernizations". They have decided not to rely on the widespread translation of materials from other languages into Chinese; but rather that the Chinese people should acquire the ability to work effectively in the necessary foreign language(s), a policy decision of immense implication for educators.

United States

There is no "official" language in the United States although English has achieved de facto status (see Gray & Tucker, 1979). English serves as the major medium of instruction for children participating in formal public education. However, in a far-reaching landmark decision (*Lau* vs. *Nichols*, see Teitelbaum & Hiller, 1977) the Supreme Court upheld the contention of a Chinese family that their child was denied access to equal educational opportunity because he did not speak English sufficiently to be able to profit from instruction in that language. Subsequently, guidelines have been issued by the federal government which state that special educational provisions must be made whenever there are 20 or more pupils within a local educational agency who share the same (non-English) mother tongue. This had led to the widespread development of mainly transitional education programs for many of the country's non- or limited English-speaking youngsters.

Although responsibility for educational matters is a state prerogative, the federal government nonetheless has a powerful influence on local practice because of the dependency of most state or local education agencies on federal funds for program operation. Nevertheless, the development of curricula, selection of textbooks, training and certification of teachers remain a state concern. Approximately 13% of the population of the United States aged 4 or older is estimated to live in households in which languages other than English are spoken (Waggoner, 1976). Of these, the Spanish-speaking constitute the largest group (approximately 40%) and they represent an extremely important political force in the United States. Bilingual education is viewed as an important tool for introducing non- or limited English-speaking youngsters to formal schooling in their mother tongue to capitalize on their state of cognitive development by introducing readiness activities, concept development, and basic content material in a familiar language while English is being added as a second language.

Canada in comparison

On the basis of this brief look at language and educational policy in selected countries, the following statements and predictions can be made about directions for Canada's educational policy.

1. Canada, like the Cameroons, is officially a bilingual country with French and English as the designated languages. Unlike many countries surveyed, federal or national policy in Canada does not extend to the prescribing and proscribing of languages to be used for public instruction. The existence within Canada of diametrically opposed and conflicting federal and provincial language policies (for example, Bill 101 in the province of Quebec and the provisions of the Charter of Rights and Freedom accompanying Canada's Constitution) is not found in the other countries surveyed. The existence of such conflicting policy is likely to result in increasing personal anxieties and social tension in Canada.

2. The provinces in Canada similar to the states of Nigeria and the United States guard jealousy their prerogatives over educational matters. The Canadian government seems not to attempt to exercise nearly so much influence, however, over educational matters as the American government. The federal government in Canada has allocated large scale funding to support second language teaching programs, but it does so by allocating the money to provinces on a per capita basis for disbursement to local educational agencies. The USA federal government, in contrast, established a reasonably complex system of disbursing funds to local educational agencies who were able to meet criteria established by it. The impact is that education in the United States will probably become more and more standardized and susceptible to ever increasing federal control with a subsequent decrease in responsiveness to local needs. This is not viewed as happening in the near future in Canada.

3. Neither Canada nor its provinces have policies which require or encourage the teaching of languages other than the official languages *to the same degree* as is the case in Jordan, Nigeria and China. Even the United States has lately come to realize the value of such language study and has established a presidential commission (similar to a Royal Commission) on the teaching of foreign languages and international studies (see Perkins, 1979). The report of that commission led to the creation of a National Council on Foreign Language Teaching and International Studies. A good deal of discussion has ensued concerning the necessity to develop and implement a "language agenda" for all Americans (Focus, 1982).

4. The population of Canada is extremely heterogeneous with large numbers of, to name but a few, Italians, Germans, and Ukrainians among its citizenry, as well as an increasingly large number of Indochinese refugees. It is inevitable that groups with established political bases will agitate increasingly for instructional programs in their languages to ensure the development of literacy and to assist in the transmission of their values, attitudes,

and traditions. Furthermore, as increasingly large numbers of school age Indochinese refugees are admitted, more and more attention will have to be given to the establishment of Vietnamese, Hmong, Chinese, and other transitional bilingual programs. Although there is occurring an overwhelming move toward vernacular language education in many parts of the world (e.g. Hartford *et al.*, 1982; Richmond, 1982) it is not at all certain that this multiplicity of educational offerings is affordable, let alone cost-effective (Heyneman, 1979). Nor can one be convinced by the empirical evidence collected to date that the manipulation of the language factor is the crucial variable in determining the relative efficacy of various pedagogical approaches (Dutcher, 1982; Tucker, 1977).

> "No uniform recommendation (such as the UNESCO Vernacular Language Axiom) can be made that will suffice for all pupils. The available empirical evidence do not permit universal generalizations. Rather, they highlight the fact that the constellation of social and attitudinal variables interact in unique ways in diverse sociolinguistic settings to affect the child's ultimate level of linguistic development." (Tucker, 1977: 40)

Canadian provinces will come under increasing pressure to develop minority language educational programs in the years ahead and should consider carefully the costs and benefits which will accrue from doing so.

5. One of the more remarkable features about the Canadian French immersion programs (see Genesee, Chapter 3) has been the extremely active and prominent role that parents have played in demanding and then helping to shape innovative, responsive language education programs. The same degree of parental involvement has not been noted in other countries surveyed. This involvement by Canadian parents has produced extremely positive effects but also an attitude has developed that the school should bear primary if not full responsibility for the second language education of the citizenry. This is a very negative consequence for if a language is to be learned well, if it is to become a tool providing access to culture, technology, and new friendships, it must be used in a variety of contexts with diverse interlocutors for varied purposes. Individuals must have the opportunity, and indeed be encouraged, to use the target language outside of the classroom. Unless some way can be found to encourage this extracurricular use of language, immersion programs will not realize their full potential as innovative language-teaching programs. A corollary of this, of course, is that attention *must* be given, within the context of formal education, to mixing Anglophone, Francophone or other mother tongue children in

classes for at least a portion of each school day to facilitate peer group language tutoring in naturalistic settings.

Conclusions

Many countries, developing as well as industralized, are moving toward universal education with at least some portion of that education occurring in the children's non-official indigenous languages. This movement is occurring in the absence of studies of the cost-effectiveness or lasting cumulative impact of such innovation, but is nevertheless likely to continue and to intensify. Many Canadian provinces have, during the past decade, developed effective programs to improve the teaching of French as a second language, but there remains room for improvement so that the second language will become a vehicle for actual communication rather than remain a subject taught intensively and exclusively at school. Likewise, in Canada, pressure will increase to develop education programs in minority languages.

An intent of this chapter has been to suggest that the Canadian situation is not at all unique and that our educational planners should seek advice, consultation and assistance from others in grappling with this task. It is important to note in this regard that much of the expertise is to be found not in the industrialized nations but rather in the developing countries discussed herein.

References

ALATIS, J. E. (ed.) 1978, International dimensions of bilingual education. *Georgetown University round table on languages and linguistics.* Washington D.C.: Georgetown University Press.

BRANN, C. M. B. (ed.) 1978, Language instruction in a multi-cultural setting. *International Review of Education*, 24, 3 (special number).

DUTCHER, N. 1982, *The use of first and second languages in primary education: Selected case studies.* Washington, D.C.: The World Bank (Staff Working Paper 504).

ENGLE, P. L. 1975, The use of vernacular language in education. Papers in applied linguistics, Bilingual Education Series: 3. Arlington, Va.: Center for Applied Linguistics.

FEDERAL REPUBLIC OF NIGERIA. 1977, *National policy on education.* Lagos: Federal Ministry of Information.

FOCUS. 1982, *A new direction for bilingual education in the 1980s.* National Clearinghouse for Bilingual Education. March.

GRAY, T. C. & TUCKER, G. R. 1979, Language policy and the delivery of social services in Canada and the United States. In J. E. ALATIS & G. R. TUCKER (eds), *Georgetown University round table on languages and linguistics.* Washington, D.C.: Georgetown University Press.

HARRISON, W., PRATOR, C. & TUCKER, G. R. 1975, *English-language policy survey of Jordan*. Arlington, Va.: Center for Applied Linguistics.

HARTFORD, B., VALDMAN, A. & FOSTER, C. R. (eds) 1982, *Issues in international bilingual education: The role of the vernacular*. New York: Plenum Press.

HEYNEMAN, S. 1979, *Instruction in the mother tongue: The question of logistics*. Washington, D.C.: The World Bank. April.

LEWIS, E. G. 1976, Bilingualism and bilingual education: The ancient world to the renaissance. In J. A. FISHMAN (ed.), *Bilingual education: An international sociological perspective*. Rowley, Mass.: Newbury House.

MACKEY, W. F. 1967, *Bilingualism as a world problem*. Montreal: Harvest House.

PERKINS, J. A. 1979, *Strength through wisdom: A critique of U.S. capability*. Washington, D.C.: The President's Commission on Foreign Language and International Studies.

RICHMOND, E. 1982, *New directions in language teaching in sub Saharan Africa*. Georgia Institute of Technology.

SOCIOLINGUISTIC SURVEY TEAM. 1979, A sociolinguistic profile of urban centers in the Cameroons. Working paper, University of Yaounde, Department of English.

TEITELBAUM, H. & HILLER, R. J. 1977, The legal perspective. *Bilingual education: Current perspectives* (vol. 3). Arlington, Va.: Center for Applied Linguistics.

TUCKER, G. R. 1977, Bilingual education: The linguistic perspective. *Bilingual education: Current perspectives*. Arlington, Va.: Center for Applied Linguistics, 2, 1–40.

WAGGONER, D. 1976, NCES' survey of languages. *Linguistic Reporter*, 19, 3, 5 & 8.

11 Beyond the English and French realities in Canada: The politics of empowerment of minorities

Vincent D'Oyley
University of British Columbia

Abstract. This chapter discusses the extent to which English and French realities control Canadian bureaucracies — their organization, delivery of services, and capacity for change. In the late 1970s federal multicultural principles held out hope for development and participation to later European groups, new visible minorities from Asia and Africa, and to the aboriginal groups. The author suggests that Canadian society be viewed as a hand comprised of five "fingers". This method of categorizing would dictate a new structure as well as the responsibilities and commitment of the bureaucracies which serve and govern Canadians at all levels.

For our purposes it is important to recognize Canada's legal bilingual fact. Contemporary Canadian civil identity is now agitated as never before by the sustaining rigor of the English–French bilingualism–biculturalism and the restrictive quality of what is left and living in the Constitution as it has been institutionalized (Cairns, 1977). Adherence to Europe has been one substantial characteristic of our institutional base; another, and a powerful restraint to equity in Canadian multi-ethnicity has been a lack of respect for new world peoples and new world forms, and especially for new world languages. This lack in the nation's traditions is a major structural crack left frequently with inadequate plaster or other remedy.

Bilingualism in the Canadian state has meant more than the emphasis on two specific languages. When in his speech on national television, 24

November 1976, Prime Minister Trudeau stated that "history created this country from the meeting of two (foreign) realities, the French and the English realities", he spoke not only about languages. He spoke then with an understanding of the myriad institutions and bureaucracies established from the perspectives of those two realities and maintained through strategems and persuasions with their roots deep in those same two European traditions.

Yet those institutions have subsequently been somewhat contextualized! As the Prime Minister spoke in 1976, the shift from the bilingualism–biculturalism of the earlier decade, a movement assisted greatly by the Royal Commission on Bilingualism and Biculturalism of that period, was already well under way. It is the most recent contextualization of official policy that we recognize as multiculturalism. We should examine components of this construct and if they are inadequate, strive for pragmatic and reasoned redefinitions. In so doing it is important to be mindful of the continual struggle for dominance within the official duality itself and also of the clash between the duality, and "the ethnics" and other minorities.

Multiculturalism

In October 1971, the Liberal government offered a formal restatement of its main policy. Seven years later, Norman Cafik, Minister of State for Multiculturalism, in speaking on *The Nation's Business* (January 8, 1978), affirmed that same policy of multiculturalism and offered a few explanations. For Cafik that policy

> "was pragmatic realization . . . that Canada is more than English and French (since) over a third of (Canadians) . . . come from backgrounds and origins other than those two fundmental groups." (p. 1)

> "meant that all Canadians . . . should be free to be able to preserve the best of their past so that they can fully develop themselves as individual human beings in a free society . . . (and) to be able to share those cultural traditions with all Canadians in an integrated society." (p. 1)

> "decreed that every policy of government takes into account the cultural diversity of our country. In matters of external affairs . . . in the question of immigration . . . in the subject of reunification of families; or in citizenship — that those very legitimate concerns of a third of our people, are taken into account by the cabinet when they make their decisions." (p. 3)

Cafik was cogent and precise about the benefits of multiculturalism for Canada and the instrumentality for achieving its objectives even when he gave the maiden address at the official opening of Multicultural Week to the Hamilton and District Multicultural Council in September 1977. Multiculturalism was to

> "formalize the preservation of many cultures from which the . . . English and French, really stand to gain more than (the others)."
> (pp. 1–2)

In that way the bilingual or French–English question would no longer be the focus of government policy. Thus, the agitation of Canadian life over language and ethnicity was being widened.

The first vision of Canadian multiculturalism reached its apogee under Cafik in 1977–1978 and saw many provinces establish their own multicultural policy. British Columbia (as evidenced by its funding of a special conference in Vancouver, April 1979) was moving toward its own multicultural statement.

But did Cafik really understand what Canadians expected from multicultural policy? For many, especially from the Anglophone–Francophone duality, the Liberals had gone too far. For numerous others, probably many from the third force, the Liberals had supplied a dream, but the fulfillment was absent. For a myriad of reasons, the Liberals, as evidenced by the 1979 federal election results, lost their grip; the people voted in a Conservative government with strong Canada West and Ontario support. Was that result further evidence of Wilson's (1974) contention that ethnicity appears to be the main independent variable affecting Canadian voting behaviour?

What then did the multiculturalism of the 1970s achieve, and where did it run into road blocks? A primary difficulty was the unwillingness of the Anglophone–Francophone duality to move clearly away from a struggle between themselves, a struggle for the right to political, economic and linguistic domination. They have not accepted "ethics" as viable entrants into a troika to influence bureaucratic reform. They had, however, made progress in bilingualizing the public service, a long overdue departure. For Francophones the "new" policy would have been non-threatening only if French (as official) language rights outside "sovereign" Quebec had been quickly enshrined and if the implementation had included provisions for a legal rearrangement that codified the official founding status of the French language. Even the less militant Acadians have seen the issue without complexity. Comeau (1979) put forth the Acadian case when he wrote:

"The rejection of multiculturalism by the Acadian community for their own development should not be interpreted as a condemnation of the policy for other ethno-cultural groups. . . . We cannot endorse, for the linguistic development of our people, a policy of bilingualism which has special considerations and safeguards for language, and at the same time endorse a policy which provides no special status for the development of the French language . . . (with guarantees for implementation). . . . At the political level . . . (there) must be . . . in each province . . . the adoption of French as an official language with the attendant consequence of irrevocable commitment." (1979: 40)

As a prelude to understanding Francophone disenchantment with multiculturalism in contemporary Canada, it should be unnecessary for us to analyse the demands of René Levesque and the Parti Quebecois, re-elected in April 1981, for sovereignty for Quebec. The gentle Acadians present the Francophone case adequately. Yet English Canada hardly comprehends the grit of current Francophone resolve to attain the "irrevocable commitment".

The Third Force

It is essential to isolate the concerns and demands of European Canadians outside of the Anglophone–Francophone reality. One must also identify the response which the third force has been receiving from the Anglophone and Francophone.

Here a rather strong ethnic pressure for improved bureaucratic response under multiculturalism has come from the Ukrainians in the Prairie Provinces although numerical strength alone would probably have suggested a German pressure instead.[1] Grygier (1977) in his Toronto study pointed out that 90% of the German group and 90% of the Dutch group attended English classes before emigrating, and he reminds us that according to Anthony Richmond a knowledge of English prior to immigration to Canada promotes cognitive acculturation. This feature and other historical circumstances and relationships could be containing the pressures from groups such as the German and Dutch in many locations in this country.

Before their advent to Canada, Ukrainians, in contrast to northwestern Europeans, had only minimal contact with the English–French duality. That relationship was a distant one. Like some other eastern Eastern groups on the Prairies, however, the Ukrainians, long before 1971, held a notion of bilingualism that was a true precursor to some central features of current multiculturalism: (a) a traditional fierce retention of their mother tongue along with the acquisition of one of the two official languages, namely English; and (b) a rigorous adherence to a life style particularized for preserving their cultural and folk traditions. These two features have made the successful Ukrainian-way a beacon for other groups in the third force who either because of size, circumstance of access to Canada, or unsustained tenacity cannot under multiculturalism yet exhibit products comparable to (a) the Canadian Institute of Ukrainian Studies, (b) a strong professional teachers group, (c) solidarity and a special culture in spite of increased urbanization for a large sector of its population, and (d) a decided influence in the federal-provincial spheres. The key is the extent to which their microstructures have been able to keep their "enclaves" dynamic (Kapelos, 1978).[2]

The visible minorities under multiculturalism

Canadian visible minorities fall into two distinct groups: the aboriginal or first peoples and the later visibles of African and Asian descent.[3]

The Aboriginal peoples

It is inconceivable that anyone, especially a Canadian educator, could be unaware of the aboriginal presence, and the history of mistransactions from which these people have, since the days of early contact, suffered in their dealings with the militarily and politically superior Europeans. The BNA Act had established federal responsibility for Indian lands and Indians, and in 1939 the Supreme Court of Canada stipulated that Eskimos were similar to Indians so far as some intents of the Indian Act were concerned. Although both aboriginal peoples have fallen under federal jurisdiction, the administration of their affairs has not been identical, and their claims on the federal government are therefore somewhat dissimilar.

Canadian history texts have traditionally tended to ignore or otherwise mistreat the aboriginal presence. In the 1970's their struggle remained inadequately represented and analyzed, with too little compassion for the areas of their ingenuity and strength. In the 19th century their frustration was even higher than it is now. As Jacqueline Gresko (1979) reminds us:

"in the 1870's and 1880's, government officials and missionaries . . . sought to pull the Indian youths out of the tribal way of life of their elders and to immerse these youths in the arts and industries of Christian civilization in industrial schools." (1979: 85)

Gresko sees a parallel between native disenchantment with Indian education, and white settler unhappiness with immigration, lands, tariff and railway when the west was being shaped. The neglect of the native social and educational condition remains unabated even now as the trend of natives to become migrants into urban Canada accelerates.

Yet one consequence of the multicultural 1970s has been a willingness by the bureaucracies, federal and provincial, to give more cognizance to the aboriginal peoples' will to speak out about their survival and to reconceptualize their strategies. The aborigines themselves have been re-examining earlier treaties (e.g. Sanders, 1973) and pressing land and fishing claims and other aboriginal demands (e.g. Joseph, 1979a, 1979b). They have given new meaning and plausibility to the phrase "aboriginal rights". More of the Canadian formal institutions have been making their programs more welcoming for aborigine students, and a few professional schools have devoted additional program energies to guide the study and adaptation of rural native Canadians who enrol as students. In many areas, too, the special boarding arrangements for native students are all but phased out. Thus some of the minor accommodations due half a century ago have flowered under the multiculturalism of the 1970s.

The structural adjustments, such as those insisted on by Berger (1977) in his report of the Mackenzie Valley pipeline inquiry and Thomas' & McIntosh's (1977) call for programs of empowerment, have not been taken seriously. The Nisghas of the Nass valley have had some success and could point the way to a cultural recovery and autonomy through these means. They now emphasize bilingualism-biculturalism in the school; their language, tradition, and culture in the home; and Nisgha riches of their land. They have effectively used the courts to gain beneficent federal response to aboriginal rights and to challenge the multinational invasion of their environment (The Nishgas and the Anglican Church vs. Amex Corporation, 1981). In recommending against the pipeline, Berger said

> "the pipeline if it were built now would do enormous damage to the social fabric of the North, would bring only limited economic benefits and would stand in the way of a just settlement of native claims. It would exacerbate tension." (1977, Vol. 1: 200)

Federal and provincial authorities are now engaging in dialogue with the Canadian native peoples more frequently or more readily than they did before multiculturalism. The major settlements of the 1980s between these two peoples will be a measure of whether Canada cares to formalize its preservation of aboriginal culture[4] and whether it will go as far as to implement meaningful native autonomy over activities central to native empowerment.

The later visibles

The status of the later visibles (Africans and Asians), differing much from that of the aborigines, has undergone some alteration in the last forty years. The point system of immigrant selection as started in 1967, by abolishing particular national, racial, and ethnic preference for landed immigrant status, promoted a dramatic shift in the multicultural character of the nation.

The exploits of the "black mosaic", Africans in Canada, are examined in many readily available sources (e.g. D'Oyley, 1978/82; Walker, 1980). Because of the liberalization of Canadian immigration laws, this sub-population has been so enlarged in the last quarter century that upwards of 70% of all Blacks have had but a short experience with Canada. The whole group has as one of its strong bonds the shared experience of racism and discrimination in socio-economic spheres, and the need to exert strong pressure especially in two of the country's oldest black regions (Halifax-Dartmouth and Windsor/Toronto areas) in a struggle against public and estabishment obstacles for fair employment, accommodation, and human rights. The urban multi-ethnic dilemma is well presented in Pitman (1977).

The size of the Asian presence in Canada has seen the sharpest rise of all continental groups through immigration; it moved from 4% in 1967 to 30% in 1976. Asians (see Ujimoto & Hirabayashi, 1980), even where they diligently built the nation's railroads and worked the farms of British Columbia, have had to await the beneficent post World War II years for the withdrawal of the more overt bureaucratic discrimination practices such as no right to vote or study in higher education centres. The Canadianization of Asians in Canada has sped up particularly because of the ability of younger members of this conglomerate (e.g. the Nisei), themselves Canadian born, to assume effective modernized leadership of the groups, to associate with liberal-minded members of the duality and to utilize national-legal techniques for their protection and development.

Africans and Asians are the last of the waves influencing growth of the Canadian population. They share not only their recency but also a high visibility, twin pillars of jeopardy in the consciousness of many Canadians (see Berry, 1977; Ujimoto & Hirabayashi, 1980). Furthermore, African-Canadians and Aborigines have seen neither prolonged nor concerted efforts to eliminate the caste barriers (Cardinal, 1977; D'Oyley, 1978; Ogbu, 1978) retarding their socio-economic progress and educational attainments.

Some conclusions

When the 1970s began, the resurgence of French language emphasis and trends outside of Quebec was unmistakable. Over the last decade Francophone resistance to formal inclusion of the third force in a troika of majority race collective has made it impossible to move the policy further along what to many seemed an obvious path. In fact it is beginning to appear that within the English–French duality there is a backlash against the emergence of non-duality forces.

The reasons for the backlash should not be hard to uncover. Some lie in the nature of the government of our society. The Canadian society is managed by a series of organizations or bureaucracies geared to guiding, shaping, binding, facilitating, and yet constraining its members (Kelsey, 1978). The constitutional, legal, and operational dynamic quality of the society remains substantially an officially bilingual-bicultural one with the multicultural refinements prone to a withdrawal of commitment. To each ethnic group, the equality, the expectation of attainment, and the majesty held out by the federal multicultural banners have not been matched by programmatic seriousness on the part of the provincial governments. In the 1980–81 federal-provincial discussions on the Constitution the opposing eight premiers (Ontario and New Brunswick excepted) long and sternly resisted the inclusion of a Bill of Rights of Native Peoples in the Constitution. Many ethnic strands, in the 1970s, a decade of more relaxed interethnic relationships, began to realize, too, how difficult it was to relate to, and work with, others most like themselves ethnically, and also that many majority race-managed institutions operated with very little caring for the survival of minority individuals from some particular strands. The negative pull of racism and discrimination still limits the growth of personal relationships and the struggle "to become" on the part of many individuals who seek access to the main bureaucracies (e.g. see O'Bryan, Reitz & Kuplowska, 1976).

Federal policy on multiculturalism has heightened the level of consciousness of many groups, provided some representation in the public service from under-represented groups, reshaped expectations of delivery from bureaucracies and paved the way for renegotiations. Although it has assisted the "ethnic" press somewhat, it has not reshaped the mainstream press and media systems in dynamic structural ways. The multicultural policy has encouraged each group to believe that it is equal one to another and that representation within the main bureaucracies has had its symbolic impact, promotive of quiescence and stability in the Canadian political system (Kernaghan, 1978).

The policy exhorts, but does not as yet provide sufficiency in its plans and implementation. A first step toward this sufficiency may be attained after people have had some redresses from the 1982 new Canadian Constitution and especially so if new and structural rearrangements of substantial socio-economic import are signed with native peoples (The Charter of Rights and Freedom, 1982). The federal government is committed to hold a special constitutional conference which will include the rights of the aboriginal peoples on the agenda and will have their representatives in attendance.

The contention here is that the current federal policy will increasingly lead to entrenchment of disillusionment and nonfulfillment, and to retrograde, especially when ethnic organizations and progressive sub-bureaucracies come under increasing pressure from within and recognize the extent to which the current general goals are unrealizable and are mostly rhetorical.

In less-expansive economic times there is need to note the many ways in which the current model of multiculturalism is weak and unaccommodating to the aspirations of many already neglected "non-duality" groups.

Toward the 1980s

Canada has entered the 1980s with more of its ethnic trends possessing a heightened awareness of social justice than would have been the case without recent multicultural dialogues and interethnic research programs. But the time has come for the society to so define itself that its organizations and bureaucracies, including school systems, may be more dynamically representative, manageable, prone to redevelopment, responsive, and capable of being systematically evaluated. A parsimonious viewing of multi-ethnicity and of multicultural operations could assist towards a rearrangement for achieving these objectives of representativeness, manageability, responsiveness, and systematic evaluation.

The main rearrangement may well be constitutional and legal in nature, avoiding lesser regulations and striving for major restructuring of systems. According to Watkins (1979), the spirit of Confederation and the ingenuity of Canadian statecraft in implementing that liberal spirit clearly advises restructures.

A real difficulty in the present arrangement is the conflict between the bilingual-bicultural duality which "owns" the main bureaucracies and has established its rules, and the egalitarian notion of multicultural equality. The search should be for a dynamic reconciliation of these two features.

This writer suggests that the "hand" of Canadian society be persuaded to a recognition of its five fingers, each of which is itself a cluster, an assemblage of sub-groups. The five fingers or assemblages are (a) the Aboriginal, (b) the Anglophone, (c) the Francophone, (d) the later European, and (e) the later visible minority or African/Asian.

The parsimony of this grouping is self-evident, and this framework may be acceptable to both English and French realities which, because of their joint proprietorship of the main bureaucracies, will be under increasing pressure to complete major settlements with the first peoples. Some structural recognition of the "hand" should hold more than face validity for the aboriginal group itself and could be palatable to both the later Europeans and Afro-Asians, if each of these two groups can itself contain intergroup squabbles within such an arrangement.

This model offers a revitalized configuration of nodules of power to affect public policy; it will realistically foster an emphasis on values other than simply accountability (see Kernaghan, 1978).

Clear advantages to this suggested arrangement could include the following:

(a) It would have a positive effect on the responsiveness and assessment demanded of bureaucracies. Based on the nature of a region's societal "hand" there could emerge new logical criteria by which a bureaucracy could deal with problems and development in any one area or region.
(b) Commitment could now be made to satisfy the economic needs of some ethnic groups from one of the five main groups in recognition of the special demands of equity.
(c) Formalization of our preservation of cadres of cultures could be addressed in the long-term and on a systematic and purposive basis.
(d) Systems such as educational and correctional services would find it essential to give attention to the special requirements of a particular assemblance of ethnic groups.
(e) More meaningful forms of alternative institutional arrangements within policy choices could now be focused on.[5]

Finally, the integrative orientation of our bureaucracies will be furthered more by the "hand" approach, rather than by the current smorgasbord view of Canadian society; and in time more citizens and groups will recognize that the hand is more than the sum of its fingers. Such a realization is essential in the realignment of group relationships and of federal-provincial policies and implementations. The major hurdle to be crossed lies in successful persuasion of the provincial levels to see primacy outside of the duality for setting societal objectives and managing the multicultural state.

Notes to Chapter Eleven

1. In the 1971 census the population (percentage) of the four main groups on the Prairies were the following:

	Anglo	French	German	Ukrainian
Alberta	46.8	5.8	14.2	8.3
Saskatchewan	42.1	6.1	19.4	9.2
Manitoba	41.9	8.8	12.5	11.6

2. Georgia Kapelos (1978) gives an excellent discussion of criteria for estimating the strength (numbers, organizational leadership style, number of organizations in a community, role of church, role of home country, etc.) of an ethnic group and that apparent relationship to grant acquisition under multiculturalism in one city (Toronto 1972–1977). Invariably strong according to her criteria and examination of fiscal data were Blacks, Italians, Jews, and Ukrainians.

3. The dilemma of Blacks under multiculturalism is discussed in D'Oyley (1978). The Asian Canadian dilemma can be easily understood after a perusal of data in (a) Graham Johnson, Ed Wickberg and William Willmott, "Chinese Canadian History Project" (published and unpublished materials, UBC Library), and (b) Japanese Canadian Manuscript Collection, UBC Archives.

4. It is unfortunate that the federal government is moving toward granting mining rights to the corporation Petro Canada for northern lands before the aboriginal rights question has been settled. This has aggravated native peoples' distrust of the official government and led to their serving notice in 1981 to bring a case against the federal government for aboriginal settlements — based partly on statutes of 1763 and 1838 — to the Chancery Division of the British High Court.

5. The policy of quiet consistency of Canada's Public Service Commission which is lauded by Wilson & Mullins (1978) could be redeveloped under the model proposed here.

References

BERGER, T. 1977, *Northern frontier, northern homeland: The report of the Mackenzie Valley Pipeline Inquiry* (2 vol.). Ottawa: Ministry of Supply and Services.

BERRY, J. 1977, *Multiculturalism and ethnic attitudes in Canada*. Ottawa: Ministry of Supply and Services.

CAIRNS, C. 1977, The Living Canadian Constitution. In J. MEEKISON (ed.), *Canadian federalism: Myth or reality* (3rd Ed.). Agincourt, Ontario: Methuen Publications.

CANADA, MINISTER OF STATE FOR MULTICULTURALISM. 1977, Official Opening of Multicultural Week '77. Sponsored by the Hamilton and District Multicultural Council. Hamilton, Ontario. September 29.

— 1978, The Nation's Business — CBC Television Program. January 8.

CANADA, PRIME MINISTER'S OFFICE. 1976, Transcript of the Prime Minister's Address on National Television and Radio. November 24.

CARDINAL, H. 1977, *The rebirth of Canada's Indians*. Edmonton, Alberta: Hurtig.

COMEAU, P. 1979, Multiculturalism and bilingualism at the community level. In A. MCLEOD (ed.), *Multiculturalism, bilingualism and Canadian institutions*. Toronto: University of Toronto.

CONSTITUTION ACT. 1982, *The charter of rights and freedom*. Ottawa: Government of Canada.

D'OYLEY, V. 1978, Schooling and ethnic rights. In H. BERKELEY (ed.), *Children's rights: Legal and educational issues*. Toronto: Ontario Institute for Studies in Education.

— (ed.), 1978 (abridged and reissued 1982), *Black presence in multi-ethnic Canada*. Toronto and Vancouver: OISE and U.B.C. Centre for the Study of Curriculum and Instruction.

— (ed.), 1982, *Perspectives on race, education and social development: Emphasis on Canada*. Vancouver: University of British Columbia, Centre for the Study of Curriculum and Instruction.

GRESKO, J. 1979, White 'rites' and Indian 'rites': Indian education and native responses in the west, 1870–1910. In D. C. JONES, N. M. SHEEHAN & R. M. STAMP (eds), *Shaping the schools of the Canadian west*. Calgary, Alberta: Detselig Enterprises Limited.

GRYGIER, T. 1977, The bottom of a tilted mosaic: The Italian community in urban Canada. In R. CARLTON, L. COLLEY & N. MACKINNON (eds), *Education, change, and society: A sociology of Canadian education*. Toronto: Gage Educational Publishing Limited.

JOSEPH, S. 1979a, *After the ink dries*. Vancouver: United Native Nations.

— 1979b, *Will promises made be promises kept*. Vancouver: United Native Nations.

KAPELOS, G. 1978, Canada's multicultural policy: "A fair play for all". An analysis of the grants distribution as a reflection of policy statement adhering to the principles of fairness and justice. M.A. thesis, McMaster University.

KELSEY, J. 1978, Structure and restructuring: Becoming uncomfortable in a comfortable world. *Education Canada*, 27–31.

KERNAGHAN, K. 1978, Changing concepts of power and responsibility. *Canadian Public Administration*, 21, 389–406.

O'BRYAN, K. G., REITZ, J. & KUPLOWSKA, O. 1976, *Non-official languages: A study in Canadian multiculturalism*. Ottawa: Department of Secretary of State.

OGBU, J. U. 1978, Minority education and caste. San Francisco: Academic Press.

PITMAN, W. 1977, *Now is not too late*. Toronto: Metro Toronto.

SANDERS, D. 1973, The Nisgha Case. *B.C. Studies*, 19, 3–20.

THOMAS, B. & MCINTOSH, G. 1977, *Return home, watch your family: A review of NITEP at UBC*. Edmonton, Alberta: Department of Indian Affairs. August.

UJIMOTO, K. & HIRABAYASHI, G. 1980, *Visible minorities and multiculturalism: Asians in Canada*. Toronto: Butterworths.

WALKER, W. 1980, *History of Blacks in Canada. A study guide for teachers and students*. Ottawa: Minister of State for Multiculturalism.

WATKINS, M. 1979, *Dene nation: The colony within.* Toronto: University of Toronto Press.

WILSON, S. 1974, Language policy. In G. DOERN & V. S. WILSON (eds), *Issues in Canadian public policy.* Toronto: Macmillan of Canada Limited.

WILSON, S. & MULLINS, A. 1978, Representative bureaucracy: Linguistic/ethnic aspects in Canadian public policy. *Canadian Public Administration*, 21, 513–38.

Index

167